JUST ADD Hormones

JUST ADD Hormones

An Insider's Guide to the Transsexual Experience

MATT KAILEY

Beacon Press
Boston

Beacon Press
25 Beacon Street
Boston, Massachusetts 02108-2892
www.beacon.org

Beacon Press books
are published under the auspices of
the Unitarian Universalist Association of Congregations.

08 07 06 05 8 7 6 5 4 3 2 1

This book is printed on acid-free paper that meets the uncoated paper ANSI/NISO
specifications for permanence as revised in 1992.

Text design by Patricia Duque Campos
Composition by Wilsted & Taylor Publishing Services

Library of Congress Cataloging-in-Publication Data

Kailey, Matt.
 Just add hormones : an insider's guide to the transsexual experience / Matt Kailey.
   p. cm.
   ISBN 0-8070-7958-8 (cloth : alk. paper)
1. Kailey, Matt. 2. Female-to-male transsexuals—United States—Biography.
3. Transsexuals. I. Title.

HQ77.8.K34A3 2004
306.76'8—dc22   2004019237

For my parents, Rod and Shirley Kailey,
who taught me a few things about humanity

contents

JUST ADD Hormones

are you Done?

I started my gender transition from female to male in 1997, after living for forty-two years as a heterosexual female in mainstream American culture. There was nothing particularly fantastical or unusual about my childhood. I grew up with a male and a female parent in a household where the father worked and the mother stayed home and raised the children. *Leave It to Beaver, Father Knows Best, I Love Lucy,* and *The Dick Van Dyke Show* were staples in our living room every night. I saw my own white, middle-class family reflected in my Dick and Jane readers, on our black-and-white Zenith, in the Saturday afternoon matinees, and in my *Highlights* magazines.

Luckily, because of my parents' own commitment to diversity, I was exposed to other races, ethnicities, and religions in our family friends, but my parents wouldn't have known about gender diversity or varying gender identities. Even differences in sexual orientation never came up in our family discussions—not because my parents would have been opposed to such discussions and not because they weren't aware that there were people in the world who weren't heterosexual. It simply didn't impact our lives.

The closest I ever came to "gay" as a child was my mother's Johnny Mathis records. I'm pretty sure now that both my parents knew he was gay—it just wasn't an issue. I seem to recall, as I got older, that they were plenty disgusted with Anita Bryant, but that could have been for any number of reasons. It was never discussed. I definitely lived in a heterosexual, bi-gendered world, so when I was diagnosed with Gender Identity Disorder (GID) at age forty-two, it pretty much served to disrupt things for me, at least momentarily. But once I got used to the fact that I had a clinical diagnosis that even my parents probably wouldn't understand, I made the decision to follow through with the remedy that made the most sense to me—I went through a gender transition.

Clinically speaking, gender transition can be a little boring (imagine that). It consists of therapy, the administration of hormones, and the unpleasantness of various surgeries, all intended to change the outward appearance of the recipient, transporting him or her into the gender of comfort, or the "opposite" gender. There are still some variations within the trans community as to language. Because the terms *sex* and *gender* have been used interchangeably in our culture for so long, the semantics can get confusing. I call what I went through a gender transition or gender reassignment. I believe that I changed my outward appearance— my gender presentation—to match the gender that I felt myself to be. Because I have not physically altered my sex organs, I rarely refer to my experience as sex reassignment.

But there are many people who would call their journey a sex reassignment. A large percentage of transpeople feel that they have always been members of the "opposite" gender and that the only thing they're changing is their sex, so that their body can live harmoniously with their mind—a sex reassignment. Some of us still use sex reassignment and gender reassignment interchangeably. Each person has his or her own name and description for what he or she went through, and for my purposes, when I speak of a gender transition or gender reassignment, I'm talking about any number of physical changes brought on by hormones, surgery, or both. For those who want a clearer idea of what various terms mean to me when I use them, there are definitions to be found at the end of this book.

Physical transition doesn't happen overnight or over the course of a weekend. Some nontranspeople assume that a female enters a hospital on Friday night and emerges Monday morning as a fully developed and fully functional adult male. I wish I knew where that hospital was. Although some of the physical changes seen in female-to-male transsexuals (FtMs) that are brought on by testosterone are irreversible, such as facial and body hair and elongated vocal cords, it must be taken for a lifetime to maintain a male pattern of body fat distribution and male muscle develop- ment, as well as the "feeling" of maleness that is a necessity for most transmen. Chest surgery does occur in a few hours, with a varying recovery time, but certain genital surgeries require sev- eral trips to the hospital over a period of several months or years, depending on finances and complications. And most transmen opt for a hysterectomy, if possible.

Because testosterone is such a strong hormone, male-to- female transsexuals (MtFs) usually take a testosterone blocker along with estrogen, at least until they've had genital surgery, if that's desired and affordable. And although estrogen causes some breast development, many transwomen opt for breast augmenta- tion. Electrolysis for the removal of facial and body hair is often an important first step for transwomen, and some have vocal cord surgery to soften and raise the voice. Because it's easier to form fe- male genitalia than it is to create a penis, genital surgery for male- to-female transsexuals is usually less complicated and much less expensive than it is for female-to-males.

Transition is a process, not a product, and spans a period of time that's usually decided by a transsexual's desires and bank account. A question I'm frequently asked when I "come out" as a transsexual is "Are you done?" As if I were a Thanksgiving turkey, the assumption is that there is a specific ending date when the little bell on the timer dings and I can then proclaim to the world that I am male. Most people who ask this question believe that transition ends with genital surgery and that no one is "done" until this is complete. There are even some laws that use genital surgery as a marker of a completed transition. In reality, "done" has more to do with the person undergoing the transition than it does with a specific time frame or set of circumstances. Some transsexual people never have surgery and are satisfied with the results of hormones alone. Others opt only for certain surgeries, such as chest reconstruction, but reject others, such as genital surgery.

There are many reasons why a transsexual might not undergo every medical option available. Some surgeries are very expensive and, since insurance rarely covers any part of a transition, at least in the United States, are simply not affordable for most people. Some people don't want to undergo multiple surgeries because of the risks or the pain involved. Certain health conditions prevent the taking of hormones or prevent certain surgeries. And although there are transsexual people who feel that they will never be "whole" unless the body has been completely changed, there are others who don't feel the need to be what our culture considers "totally male" or "totally female." The feeling of "doneness" that exists in any transsexual's mind might be completely at odds with what a nontransperson considers a finished product.

And physical changes are only part of a transition. They don't prepare a person to function adequately in a gender in which he or she wasn't socialized. Socialization is often a massive barrier that's difficult to overcome. In some cases, a transsexual person must literally be taught how to function in his or her "new" gender—how to walk, talk, sit, stand, and interact with others as a member of that gender—things that were learned by nontranspeople in childhood and adolescence. Some transpeople spend a great deal of time learning these new behaviors, while to others they come naturally. Then there are some who are simply unconcerned with how "male" or "female" they appear in their new roles.

Comfort with one's body and a congruity between body and mind are the goals of transition, and these concepts mean different things to different people. For some, a mixture of the masculine and feminine body types, behaviors, and thought processes is sufficient. For others, only a complete and all-inclusive transition to the "opposite" gender will do.

For all the problems that transsexual people have in transitioning to the "opposite" gender, it seems to me that the use of the term *opposite* in this context might signal a societal misconception that affects not just transpeople but everyone. When we use the term, we're automatically setting up a strict binary gender system (a two-gendered system) that leaves no room for anyone who doesn't specifically conform, physically and emotionally, to what our society considers either "male" or "female." Intersexed people are one example of this. There are many ways that a body can be configured—including various chromosomal and genital structures—that differ from the standard female and male body types in some way. The Intersex Society of North America's Web site (http://www.isna.org) provides information on the many ways that human bodies can differ. These differences are not always obvious and don't necessarily interfere with living in a binary gender system, but might have serious implications when talk turns to chromosome testing for marriage licenses or how many inches make an "acceptable" penis. If we have only "opposite" genders, where do intersexed people fit in? And this doesn't even take into account the tens of thousands of people with transsexual bodies— bodies that have been altered by hormones, surgery, or both.

The term *opposite* establishes permanent polarity, with no room to move between genders, to adopt characteristics of both male and female genders, or to identify as something else entirely. There's little room to maneuver in such a state of opposites, and even nontransgendered people often have trouble subscribing to all the roles and expectations that are assigned to their gender. However, the pressure to do so is immense, since to diverge puts a person at odds with, or "opposite" of, the rest of society.

But the term is firmly embedded in our culture. Like a pesky houseguest, it has made itself quite at home and shows no signs of leaving (or cleaning up the bathroom). Even I use it, to my own dismay, because I'm no less a product of the binary gender system than anyone else. The notion that transsexual people are somehow immune to the strict gender roles and expectations prescribed by our society is simply not correct. Many transpeople subscribe to these roles far more fervently than nontransmen and -women do. It's a way of finally feeling comfortable with their gender, their sex, and their place in society.

I underwent a gender transition and lived to tell about it (most of us live; fewer of us tell about it). I take male hormones (pharmaceutical testosterone) by intramuscular injection and will take them for the rest of my life. I've had chest surgery. I've legally changed my name and my identification papers. I've lived in society as a female and as a male—and for a very brief time as something no one could seem to identify. There's not as much difference as people who have lived as only one or the other might think.

Certainly, I've noticed differences. As a female, I was afraid to walk after dark and, when I had to, I was quite aware of who was behind me, in front of me, and on either side, as well as which houses had porch lights on and where I might find safe refuge if necessary. Now, after transition, I rarely worry. I am, however, more likely to get shot, more likely to be involved in a physical fight, and more likely to be expected to intervene in someone else's fight. I am also now expected to lift heavy objects and change my own flat tires. Other men speak to me in a way, and with language, that they never did when I was female. I'm told I have "male privilege," but I was never socialized to expect it and wouldn't know what it was if it was handed to me wrapped with a big blue bow. But I also know now that men feel the same insecurities that women do, that men and women have many of the same needs and wants, and that if people in general were taught to open up to each other, we would probably, for the most part, get along just fine.

Transsexuals are the ones who can change gender as we know it. We are the ones who can liberate not only ourselves but the rest of society from the strict cultural standards that are almost impossible for anyone to meet. For women who have tried and failed to measure up to the airbrushed fantasies in glossy men's magazines, for men who measure "success" by both muscular bodies and muscular bank accounts and fail to "succeed" at either one, wouldn't it be nice to take a deep breath and just say, "Forget it"? Transsexual people have little choice, and so, eventually, many of us do just that. And in the midst of that overwhelming freedom, we forge ahead and form our lives—the lives that we were meant to live. Welcome to mine.

PART ONE

Trans Minds

we're everywhere

Besides being your family, friends, neighbors, and coworkers, transfolk are basically just people. Boring, isn't it? We pay taxes, we go to work (if we're lucky enough to be in supportive employment situations), we go shopping (if we're employed), we eat, we sleep. We're pretty much like everybody else, although we often tend to consider ourselves infinitely more interesting.

It's difficult to determine how many transgendered people there are in the world, primarily because most people whose gender identity doesn't match their physical body or who choose to express their gender in a way that's not in line with mainstream culture never come to the attention of those who gather statistics. It's certainly not a question I've ever seen on a census form. And transsexual people, those who change their physical bodies to match their gender identity, are only a small part of the transgendered or gender-diverse population. Transsexual people are slightly easier to track, because they usually do come to the attention of medical professionals, but even then, many travel great distances, sometimes overseas, to have surgery, and some get hormones over the Internet or from other sources that aren't so easily documented.

In the grand scheme of trans counting, the numbers simply aren't clear, even in professional communities. And the general population's perception of us is way off base. The average nontransperson's idea of a transsexual is actually closer to a drag queen—a man who dons women's clothes for entertainment purposes. This "man in a dress" stereotype doesn't even come close to the typical transsexual person living his or her life in today's world. And it doesn't take into account at all the legions of female-to-male transsexuals out there. Transmen simply aren't on anyone's radar screen.

There really aren't more MtF transsexuals than there are FtMs. Recent statistics have shown that the numbers are about equal. However, there are several reasons why it *appears* that there are more MtFs than FtMs. Because statistics about the number of transsexual people in existence have historically been gathered by psychiatrists, physicians, and surgeons who work with trans populations, FtMs have been underestimated. It's far easier for a female to live in society as a male without any hormones or surgery than vice versa. In the past, and probably still, many transgendered females have opted to simply present themselves as men and live their lives as men rather than seek help through therapeutic and medical intervention. Therefore, they haven't come to the attention of statistics gatherers.

It's also far easier for a transgendered female to live as a masculine female, dressing in men's clothing, wearing a male hairstyle, and generally presenting in a masculine way than it is for a male to wear a dress, high heels, and a wig. Masculine females are far more accepted in our culture than feminine males. Therefore, some transgendered females have chosen to remain in a female role with the accoutrements of masculinity rather than undergo hormone treatments and surgeries, which always have risk. Transgendered males, on the other hand, are not allowed such a "luxury," so have transitioned instead.

And it's been only recently that transgendered females have had transsexual female-to-male role models to emulate. Christine Jorgensen and Renee Richards were early and well-known male-to-female pioneers who provided models for other MtFs to follow. Now that there are visible FtM transsexuals in the media and elsewhere, transgendered females are aware of what's available to them and are beginning to take advantage of their options.

Also, testosterone is a very powerful hormone that overcomes estrogen quickly, making it easy for FtMs to assimilate rapidly into mainstream male society. FtMs are usually unrecognizable as such on the street. Beards, low voices, male pattern baldness, and muscle growth all serve to create a presentation that is decidedly and unmistakably male. This ease of assimilation makes it very tempting for transmen to leave their pasts behind and to cease to identify as transsexual at all. Their new neighbors and friends don't know. FtMs may appear as shorter than average males with slightly wider hips and butts, but there are so many nontransmales who are shorter than average that it's usually not an issue. And I've seen butts on some nontransguys that would rival those of even the heftiest of transmen.

MtFs have a more difficult time with assimilation. They are often much taller than the average female, with a much larger build and larger hands. Facial hair is often noticeable, and electrolysis is time-consuming and expensive. The shape and size of the skull are sometimes issues, as is muscle development, which tends to soften with estrogen but sometimes doesn't entirely go away. Vocal cords are lengthened by testosterone, but once elongated, they don't shrink up, even under the influence of estrogen, so MtFs must work hard to master a higher-pitched voice or have surgery to alter it. For those with very low voices, it can be difficult. Although countless MtFs have successfully assimilated into mainstream female society, it can be a much more complex and tedious process than it is for FtMs. Because of these difficulties, more MtFs make use of resources such as gender centers and support groups than do FtMs, who tend to use these resources for initial support, then disappear into the mainstream once testosterone works its magic. But the scales are balanced, because FtM surgery is far more expensive and the results are less satisfactory.

Socialization is also an issue. Men are socialized to speak out, to be visible, to press for what they need. Women are taught just the opposite. That socialization often carries over after transition, making MtFs more vocal and open about who they are and what they require—and, therefore, more visible in society than FtMs.

Things are changing, however. The Internet has helped all transpeople, bringing them information that was previously un-available and offering them friendship and support where there was once only isolation. More and more FtMs are coming out and making their voices heard, becoming role models for transgen-dered females seeking gender reassignment. More doctors and surgeons are becoming aware of FtMs and are tailoring their prac-tices toward us, making FtM gender reassignment more accessi-ble. But even as opportunities open, we still carry a lot of social baggage along with us on the trip.

Most transmen will laugh, some quite loudly, at the notion that we transition in order to achieve male privilege. I've been transi-tioned for many years and still don't know what that is. I've looked around, but the concept is as elusive as the winning lottery ticket that I'm sure I purchased but now can't find anywhere. Transmen transition because of a gender incongruity, and if male privilege comes with it, it's only a side effect. But most of us will attest to the fact that there isn't much male privilege out there to be had.

A large number of transmen are in female-dominated occupa-tions and remain there even after transition, either because they don't have the education or training to move into a higher-paying, male-dominated field or because they're happy where they are—they've chosen work that suits them. It's not their fault that soci-ety devalues what it considers "women's work." I stayed in social work for many years because I was good at it and it was what I knew. Those who had children before transition are often paying child support to a former husband who used their transsexuality against them in the divorce proceedings in order to gain primary custody of the children. And if transmen *are* raising their children, they're often doing it alone and without financial assistance—in many cases because the children's father is so angered by the transition that he uses it as an excuse to neglect his offspring.

Those who are lucky enough to be in high-paying positions still have the expense of hormones and surgery, and genital surgery can run up to $60,000 or more in the United States. And no transman can take his high-paying job for granted—he can easily be fired when he begins his transition.

It's true that there are some people who look more favorably upon FtMs than they do upon MtFs. In our culture, as in many, males are held in higher esteem, so it's easier for people to accept the fact that a female would want to transition into manhood than vice versa. For those not familiar with the nature of transsexuality, it appears to be simply a step up in the world. In our misogynistic culture, MtFs are seen as taking a step down—any male who wants to be a female must be crazy. Why would a man want to give up his position in the world? In reality, that position must be awfully shaky if male-to-female transsexuals can upset so many just by moving away from it.

But transmen have their share of opposition. We're still transsexuals, after all, and that's a position that hardly goes hand in hand with societal privilege. Besides the fact that transsexuality in general is seen as disgusting and sick, quite a few nontransmen find FtMs offensive. Just as some men find lesbians threatening because they see lesbianism as a personal rejection, others are angry at transmen for the same reason—by transitioning, we have somehow, in their minds, rejected the masculine sexuality that they were able to offer us when we were female. To these men, I say, "Relax, guys. There are still plenty of women to go around. My transition is no reflection on your obvious manly hunkiness. And if you're worried that your attraction to me before my transition means you're gay—it doesn't. Trust me on that one."

Perhaps it's time to give masculinity and femininity a much-needed rest. Maybe it's time to incorporate gender diversity into our society, to let go of our white-knuckled grip on gender roles and expectations, and to remove the threats to traditional masculine and feminine appearance and behavior just by letting that tradition go. Incorporating gender diversity into our mainstream culture can do more than just make a safer and more accepting place for transpeople. It can free all people to live in the ways in which they're most comfortable.

For so long, women have been told to "act like men" in order to succeed in business and other professional fields. What if they could move up by acting in a professional manner, with no gender bias and no behavioral expectations other than hard work and competence? What if there was no such thing as "acting like a man," and people simply acted in ways that came naturally to them? What if there were no threats to masculinity or femininity because the concepts were fluid and anyone could be as "masculine" or as "feminine" as he or she wanted to be? We wouldn't be doing away with men or women—we'd just be giving everyone some breathing room.

Transsexuals are no threat to humanity. We want only what everyone else wants—to live our lives in ways that are comfortable to us, whether that means adopting more "traditional" roles or creating new ones that suit us. And as our numbers increase and we become more visible, we will hopefully have more say in the matter. Watch for us.

TEXTBOOK Transsexuals

I am not a textbook transsexual. In fact, my life experience defies almost everything ever written about transsexuals by nontranssexuals. Unfortunately, that body of information comprises most of the reference material to which doctors and therapists refer when diagnosing and working with transpeople. The *DSM*, the *Diagnostic and Statistical Manual* that is used by mental health professionals to assign labels to people who display behaviors and thought patterns considered to be "abnormal" in society, is filled with inaccurate information on transgendered folk, especially in reference to female-to-males. It's frightening to think of the transgendered females who are being misdiagnosed and mistreated at the hands of inexperienced therapists who use the *DSM* as their diagnostic bible.

I was lucky enough to encounter a therapist who had such an extensive knowledge of trans issues that she had no need to consult the dreaded manual to determine what I would need. I wasn't a tomboy, which is one of the first clues that therapists look for in diagnosing a Gender Identity Disorder in natal females. I was also not attracted to females, a significant precursor to a *DSM* diagnosis. In fact, if my therapist had followed the narrow guidelines set forth in that manual, I wouldn't be writing this today.

That the *DSM* provides erroneous diagnostic tools for professionals working with transpeople is only a symptom of a larger problem—the notion that varying gender identification is a cause for concern at all. Anyone who deviates from the behaviors, appearance, and roles that were designated to that individual by way of his or her genitalia is considered to have a mental health issue. I still have an official diagnosis—Gender Identity Disorder. It's a necessary diagnosis to get the hormones and surgeries needed for a gender transition. But I still find it amazing that, with such a debilitating mental illness as described in the *DSM*, I was able to obtain a master's degree, work in the same field for eighteen years, receive outstanding evaluations, and generally maintain my equilibrium throughout life. Is it possible that it's not the person who's dysfunctional but the culture—a culture that dictates such a narrow definition of male and female that many people simply don't fit?

The *DSM* seems to get larger and more cumbersome every time it's revised. With all the conditions that it now lists, just about everyone alive has a diagnosable mental illness. Teenagers are being diagnosed left and right with "oppositional defiant disorder." When I was younger, they called it "adolescence." Anger, sadness, fatigue, fear—all the human emotions that stem from living in the twenty-first century, or indeed from living at all—are now diagnosable conditions. And more and more people are being diagnosed with mental illness and medicated for same every day. We are all products of our culture, and maybe it's time we take a look at the world around us to figure out *why* we're angry, sad, tired, and afraid.

But is it our culture that produces Gender Identity Disorder? In a way, yes, it is. Our culture certainly doesn't *generate* whatever it is that makes a person feel out of alignment with his or her body. We still have no idea what that's all about. But our culture does stigmatize this feeling not only as unnatural but as a full-blown mental illness. Society doesn't produce the feeling, but society provides the diagnosis. And with the diagnosis comes the idea that this incongruity is somehow faulty and problematic. *We* as trans-people are faulty and problematic. But even as we are seen to have a mental illness, there is little help, or even empathy, forthcoming.

The "treatment" for Gender Identity Disorder has been documented to be, in many cases, gender reassignment—changing the body to match the mind. The reverse has been tried, time and time again, and has been unsuccessful. But the "treatment" is still considered unacceptable, isn't covered by insurance, and is generally difficult and expensive to get. We shouldn't be surprised, though. Our culture stigmatizes mental illness while continuing to add conditions to the *DSM* with increasing fervor, giving everyone in our path some kind of diagnosable disorder.

True mental illness is, in fact, a serious situation that accounts for many problems in our society, even as it lines the pockets of pharmaceutical giants everywhere. People who are truly mentally ill, or who have physiological chemical imbalances that create mental or emotional disturbances, need help, services, and most of all, compassion and understanding. But let's not add to that real problem by creating another one—wasting our precious mental health resources on people who have no mental illness. If trans-people have any emotional difficulties at all, it's likely that they stem from society's refusal to accept any appearance or behavior outside of the narrowly prescribed gender norms that have been established to keep us all—trans and nontrans alike—in line.

There's little room for diversity—what white, mainstream, heterosexual society sees as "difference"—and if that diversity dares to cross any kind of line, it's labeled as "sick" or even "perverted." In fact, no cause for body/mind gender disagreement has been determined. It's a "chicken or egg" dilemma that the medical and psychiatric communities are still trying to figure out—is transgenderism in itself a mental illness, or does any mental illness a transperson might exhibit come from society's expectations of and limitations on gender? Is there a physical component, some synapse in the brain that's firing differently or a prenatal dose of the wrong hormone? Or do people choose to be transgendered? After all, who wouldn't enjoy taking hormones throughout life, having multiple surgeries, and being rejected by society?

It could be psychological, physiological, a little of both, or simply another way of being human in the ongoing epic mystery known as life. Most transsexuals are happy, well adjusted, intelligent human beings who are functioning well in society. Our only distress, besides the day-to-day hassles of living that everyone experiences, comes from society's treatment of us. As long as we have access to services that allow us to live authentic lives as the people we truly are, we are no more or less unhappy than anyone else. But should our access to services be contingent on a diagnosis of mental illness? We can't get hormones or surgery without such a diagnosis. We're required to have letters from mental health professionals in order to begin taking hormones or receive gender reassignment surgery. And while this, in and of itself, is not necessarily a bad thing—anyone who is considering undergoing major physical and emotional changes probably needs a proper assessment, recommendations, and follow-up—it puts transpeople at the mercy of a system that believes them to be mentally ill.

Whatever the cause, gender identity is not a choice, just as sexual orientation is not a choice. Many believe that transitioning is also not a choice. If the incongruity between a person's gender identity and his or her body and social roles is strong enough, he or she will transition or die. Although quite a few transgendered individuals are able to remain in their birth sex, living part-time in the gender with which they identify or ignoring gender designations altogether, many are not.

A large number of transgendered suicides occur because people are not able to transition, for whatever reason—marriage, children, employment, finances, community, and so on. And although many people equate suicide with mental illness, many suicides are based simply on suffering. Eliminate the suffering and the desire for death is also eliminated. Those experiencing painful terminal illnesses sometimes seek out assisted suicide to relieve themselves of suffering. This isn't the result of a mental illness. If transpeople are relieved of the suffering inherent in being forced to live in the wrong gender, trans suicide rates will drop as well.

But alleviating that suffering includes access to services and, in some cases, gender reassignment. Alleviating that suffering also includes acceptance, support, and a place in society. It sounds so simple—and it could be, if our culture could come to terms with gender diversity. As it is, transpeople often have limited options available to them. Because insurance doesn't cover any aspect of a gender transition, many transpeople are prevented financially from taking even the initial steps necessary to live in their true gender. And because we can be fired from our jobs, lose our homes, families, and friends, and put ourselves in danger of assault—even murder—for transitioning, many find the risks just too overwhelming.

Minorities, who experience other prejudices as well and who are often in underpaid jobs, find it especially difficult. Youth have difficulty accessing information and support and run the risk of being kicked out of their homes and onto the streets if they come out to their parents as trans. Our culture finds transgendered and transsexual people so morally reprehensible that we, as a society, seem to prefer death (by suicide) for these individuals to appropriate medical treatment. Also, because there is such shame in our culture around anyone who deviates from the standard male/ female heterosexual identifications, it's difficult for transpeople, especially those from rural areas and small towns, to find the help they need. The Internet has been a boon for us, with its anonymity and wealth of information, but it's much more beneficial to connect face-to-face with others.

In the past twenty to thirty years, a handful of gender centers in larger metropolitan areas has had the daunting task of servicing whatever trans individuals could gain access to them. These services have focused primarily on emotional support and on providing information. Until very recently, transpeople who transitioned did so in secrecy and were urged to start new lives in their new gender and remain "in the closet" about their transness, to spare them from humiliation, assault, and even death at the hands of others who did not approve. There is, however, a trans movement under way that is becoming more and more visible and is focusing on politics rather than support, on being "out" and being heard, on changing attitudes and legislation.

Those transpeople who are "out" are demanding rights that were previously unheard of and are making names for themselves in the larger community. Unfortunately, those few in the spotlight can't do it all, and the shame and danger of being a transsexual remain. In this catch-22 situation, transsexuals will not be safe "coming out" until the popular attitude changes, and the popular attitude will not change until more and more transsexuals come out and are heard.

Attitudes toward gay men and lesbians are changing, although too slowly, as people increasingly realize that they know (and like) someone—a neighbor, coworker, relative, or even celebrity—who is gay or lesbian. When more and more people begin to realize that they also know (and like) a transperson, we will hopefully see a positive paradigm shift. We're still waiting.

PART TWO

Trans IDENTITY

WHAT'S IN A NAME?

Going through a gender transition is a bit like being born, without the scary doctors and the disorienting, headfirst trip down a suffocating tunnel. You can literally start your life over, no matter what your age, and make those important decisions that someone else made for you when you started the original trip decades ago. You're old enough to reject the idea of handing out pink or blue bubble gum cigars emblazoned with "It's a Boy" or "It's a Girl" in favor of serving the strongest liquor available at your coming-out party. You can pass on the pacifiers and satisfy your oral cravings in whatever way you choose (I stayed with cigarettes—food ranks right up there). You can skip the stifling piano lessons that your mother hoped would turn you into a toddling child prodigy in favor of the hobby that you've always dreamed about but that might have given you away, such as pro wrestling or needlepoint, depending on your original gender.

And best of all, you get to choose your own name. No longer do you need to be saddled with the moniker of your mother's favorite soap opera character. Never again will signing on the dotted line remind you of the promise your father made on his Great-Uncle Herman's deathbed. (If there's a transman out there named Herman, first, let me apologize. Second, let me ask, "What the hell were you thinking?") Now you can choose the name of your own most admired television star or your favorite dead relative. I chose

the name my parents planned to give me at birth had I been born
a boy the first time around. It's not my favorite name, but the problem with favorite names is that they tend to change when one soap
opera character dies and is replaced by a sexier, better-looking, or
smarter one. My name is a name that should have been, and that's
what makes it right.

Choosing a name is one of the earliest steps in gender transition and is the beginning of a new identity formation. But it's
definitely only the beginning. For the first year or two of my transition, I struggled with an identity crisis that seemed to eclipse the
original gender conflict that brought me to that place to begin
with. Male hormones were morphing my body into a man, someone almost unrecognizable, but my psyche still said I was me, whoever that was. And not knowing who that was turned out to be the
biggest problem. In the beginning, the face in the mirror was still
that of a female, albeit a masculine one, and the breasts, though
tied down, were still there. Although the clothing was purchased
in the men's department, the body it covered was decidedly wom-
anly. As testosterone took hold, my voice crackled like a static-
filled radio, the muscles of my upper body swelled, and the face in
the mirror began to take on hard edges and sprout hair. But the
question remained the same—"Who is that?"

We're a society of labels, and I was having a hard time finding
one that fit. Was I a man? A transman? A female-to-male transsexual? All or none of the above? My life was turning into a multiple-
choice exam. There were so many designer labels at my disposal
that I felt as if I'd taken a wrong turn and entered Saks instead of
Target. It took me a while to decide, but now, several years later, I
still use the label I selected in the beginning—transman.

To the uninitiated, it might sound like something out of a sci-
ence fiction movie, but then, so does gender transition. For those
of us who have undertaken the journey, it makes perfect sense. We
all have certain words or phrases that we use to describe ourselves

—gay, straight, transsexual, transgendered, liberal, conservative, in need of serious intervention—whatever fits us best. Many FtMs prefer to identify as "male" or "a man," leaving off the trans part entirely. That's fine if it works for them.

For me, it was a problem that I didn't recognize until it was pointed out by my therapist, who was very wise in these matters. I complained to her during one session that I felt "genderless," no longer a female but definitely not a male. I was starting to look like a man, but I still had many physical and behavioral markers that pegged me as a woman. I was floating in a gray zone, the invisible period that every transsexual is familiar with. It's that time of day between light and dark, when everything turns the uniform non-color of a miller moth. That thirty-minute layover at the airport, when your connecting flight isn't ready to board but there's not enough time to find the smoking room. Those few seconds between sleep and waking, when the alarm clock buzz could be the sound of the tornado in your dream. It's that period of time in transition when some people think you are a "ma'am," others see you as a "sir," and still others are so unsure that they sputter and stare until they finally give up and refuse to acknowledge you at all. When you have no visible gender, the whole of you becomes invisible as well—and even you start to wonder if you're really there.

It was then that I needed a label most, something to define me as more than just a blob of skin and muscle and tissue, a container for the testosterone/estrogen war that was going on inside. My therapist understood. She suggested that I was definitely not a woman, but perhaps I was not a man, either. Perhaps I was a transsexual, a transman, different from the biological male with whom I was attempting to identify. She asked me to think about what it meant to me to be a transmale. And, because I was a good patient who subscribed to the notion that people can't be helped unless they're willing to help themselves, I thought about it.

I thought about it a lot, and I decided that she was right. When

I began to think of myself as a transman, something wholly apart from either a biological male or a biological female, a different animal entirely, I no longer felt genderless. I felt transgendered, which seemed like an appropriate label to put on whatever it was that compelled me to pay someone good money to stick a needle in my rear. I finally accepted the fact that I would always be a transman, no matter how male I became, and for me, that eventually became okay.

I've discovered, in speaking with hundreds of transpeople in the last few years, that my early feeling of being "genderless" was not unique. Some actually embrace this feeling and attempt to maintain it. Others squirm, as I did, so completely socialized into our binary gender system that not connecting with a specific gender lends a feeling of rootlessness and instability. It was important for me to have some kind of gender identification, even if it was a little left of center. It made me feel better to have something to call myself, especially because I was confronted with so much ambiguity from the outside.

When I was in my gray period, panicking over my own indeterminate gender, my neighborhood grocery store clerk was going through his own brand of panic whenever I decided to brave the world and go out shopping. I noticed that he seemed overwhelmed by the desire to call me "ma'am" or "sir," but he couldn't figure out which one I was. When he thought I wasn't looking, he desperately stole glances at my face and body like a detective at a crime scene as he removed each item from my cart and slid it across the scanner. He engaged me in idle chitchat just to hear the tone of my voice. When all else failed, he examined my chest, hoping to see some protrusion or lack thereof that would give him the answer he needed.

And when the cart was almost empty, sweat formed on his brow. His hands began to shake. I was signing my debit card receipt.

There was no time left. He would have to say something—"Thanks for shopping at Food R Us, ma'am" or "Please come back again, sir." What if the boss was watching? He would surely be docked in pay if he couldn't perform so simple a closing. He would just have to guess. But what if he guessed wrong? That would be the ultimate insult, ensuring that I would never again step foot in Food R Us. I might even complain to the manager. When the trauma became overwhelming for him, I picked up my bags and left, leaving him to wonder what exactly I was.

But that was an American clerk, typical of all the American clerks that I ran into, born and bred into a stifling gender system that made no allowances for diversity. For a time, I dreaded leaving my house because it seemed that I made things so difficult for everyone around me. Maybe I could deal with this "transman" business, but what was I doing to those in the service sector? I was the stuff of salesclerk nightmares. And then I happened upon Elyse.

When I was searching for a birthday present for my sister, I found myself in a very familiar place—the women's department of the local Foley's. As I shuffled through the racks of women's clothing, a salesclerk approached from behind. Perhaps noticing my rounded hips in front of a carousel of blouses, she asked, in some kind of European accent, "Can I help you, ma'am?"

When I turned around, she blinked and said, "Oh, I mean, sir."

I couldn't tell where Elyse was from, I knew only that her accent was not of this continent. And neither was her behavior. When I smiled, a dead giveaway of female heritage, she continued unflustered.

"I'm sorry. I mean, ma'am."

"It's okay," I said.

She frowned. "I mean, sir."

"It's okay," I assured her, not wanting to go into lengthy explanations for a cheap birthday sweater. "Either is fine." I wasn't sure, at that point, if either *was* fine, but I was determined to get through the situation with as little anguish as possible for both of us.

Not satisfied, and apparently dead set on getting it right, she replied, "No, really, what are you?"

I had no answer—at least not one that I thought would suit her. I could have said, *Well, as a matter of fact, I've been discussing that very question with my therapist.* But I didn't. I just said, "It doesn't matter," then turned away and continued to shop. I had forgotten how much it really *did* matter, how I was causing her to violate every rule in the salesperson's Code of Conduct manual.

But she hadn't forgotten. When I had finally made my selections and approached her counter to pay, she studied my credit card. "Matthew," she said. "Then you're a man." She wasn't sweating. She wasn't shaking. She just wanted to know.

I liked her so much by then, simply because she wasn't upset, that I said, "I'm a transsexual."

In the United States, when particular words are spoken, like "convicted felon," "tuberculosis patient," or "transsexual," people begin to get very nervous and slowly edge away, muttering apologies until they're a safe distance away. Apparently, in whatever country Elyse was from, such things are, instead, introductions to intimate conversations. As she rang up and bagged my purchases, she launched into a complete and rather knowledgeable explanation of what male hormones would do to me as long as I continued to use them. Thanks to Elyse, I learned that my voice would soon get even lower and that, when the facial hair started, there would be no more mistakes about my gender. Of course, I knew these things, but there was nothing more comforting than having them reinforced by the salesclerk at Foley's.

After spending several minutes with this woman, I knew that I wanted her to sell me all of my clothes for the rest of my life, check out my groceries at Food R Us, and deliver my mail. I also wanted her to walk around with me every day and explain things to other people. Elyse embodied all the characteristics that I had hoped to see in my own countrymen and -women since the beginning of my transition—curiosity, honesty, and acceptance. And Elyse made me feel okay about being what I was—a transman.

Although it appeared at the time that everything was finalized, that I had tied things up with a neat little pink and blue bow and decided to move on, secure in my label, the struggle was far from over. I flopped around more than a grounded fish, trying to figure out if I was a man, or just sort of a man, or only a man on Sundays or in months that began with "J." I went out on a limb (a real short, skinny, teetery one) several times, insisting that a man was exactly what I was, only to revert eventually to the transsexual identity that I knew I would carry around, like those extra ten pounds that I gained from testosterone, for the rest of my life. But when I went through my "manly" phases, I was not to be daunted by something as trifling as transsexuality. I was "passing," being seen as male by the outside world, which was a high so heady that it beat all the drug experimentation I did in college. It was what I had been waiting for.

"Passing" plays an important role in the initial phases of transition. It's often how a transsexual person measures his or her progress on hormones. If I had a skill for invention, and if trans-people had any money, I could probably live comfortably by creating a Pass-O-Meter that would track passing percentages and come up with a grand total of how "male" or "female" an individual was seen by the world.

When I began my journey, I measured my transition—and myself—in terms of how I was perceived by people with whom I came into contact. My primary source of feedback was how often I was "sirred" as opposed to "ma'amed." If, on any given day, one out of four strangers called me "sir" instead of "ma'am," I assumed I was "passing" 25 percent of the time. As my metamorphosis continued, that percentage increased until I was finally "passing" 100 percent of the time. But by then, I no longer used the word.

The problem with "passing" is that the concept is built around the idea of deception—that a person is one way and is "passing" for something else. And as I struggled through my "manly" stages, I wanted nothing to do with "passing." I was a man. That I was a man without a penis was simply an unfortunate fact of life, like being a man without an arm or a man without an eye. The concept of "passing" assumed that I was attempting to be something I wasn't —that I was pulling a fast one on the rest of the world, getting by with some kind of false presentation. If I really was a man, then I wouldn't be "passing" for one—I would just be one.

"Passing" is actually a necessary concept in the first stages of a transition and probably shouldn't be ignored. It's a measurement of what's happening to you. Paying attention to it and talking about it psychologically reinforce what you are becoming physically. The milestone "firsts" are exciting and important—the first "sir," the first time you're directed to the men's room instead of the women's, the first time you flash your new driver's license at a club, the first time a gay man or a straight woman flirts with you. As you move through the stages, the "sirs" become commonplace and the once-in-a-while "ma'am" hits you in the face like a splash of ice water.

Then you come to a point when you start to realize that the "ma'am" never happens anymore—never ever. It hasn't happened for months. You walk into a group of men and you belong there. No one looks at you with a question in his eyes. The nurse at the ob/gyn clinic thinks you're some kind of pervert when you try to make an appointment. And the awareness sinks in—what you feel on the inside is what they see on the outside. You are a man. You're no longer "passing." You just are.

The "passing for a man" stage eventually went away, and for a brief period of time, I ignored my transman identity as much as possible and entered the "being a man" stage. This eventually went away, too, although I had to go through a lot of disillusionment to get there. I was still fighting with the man/transman dichotomy, still wavering back and forth from day to day and sometimes hour to hour about exactly who or what I might be. But the universe has a way of guiding us if we just sit back and let it take the reins. And the universe decided to throw some curves my way—or, at least, one jagged chunk of metal.

By the time I saw it, it was too late. I was cruising down I-70, hurrying to get back to work from an appointment and thinking about everything but an emergency situation, when the metal shot like a bottle rocket from under the tire of the car in front of me and right into my path. My tire deflated instantly, and I steered my hobbling car to the shoulder of the highway. The last time my car had been disabled, several years before, a total of five cars, each with a varying number of men inside, had stopped to help in the twenty minutes before my husband had arrived. *That's it,* I thought. *All I have to do is get out of the car and wait.*

I got out of the car. I waited. The sun was unbearable, and the hot air whipping off the cars passing by me at seventy miles an hour made things even more miserable. Nobody was going to stop. Who would stop to help a man? And wasn't I a man? This called for some quick thinking—some masculine thinking.

There were things in the trunk, I remembered, that were meant for just such an emergency. I dug them out one by one, consulting my owner's manual and matching up each piece with the drawing. When they were all laid out by the roadside, I read the entire manual chapter on changing a tire. Then I proceeded to try to follow the instructions.

I managed to get the jack wedged underneath the frame, and with torturous grunting and tugging, pushing and pulling, the jack handle repeatedly coming off in my hand, I got the car elevated. I figured out on my own that I could loosen the lug nuts by pounding on the lug nut loosener with my foot. But the lug nut loosener was also the lug nut tightener, and several times I made the frustrating mistake of going in the wrong direction. *Lefties, loosies; righties, tighties.* It was my mantra until I finally got the tire off. It would have been a whole lot easier if I had loosened the lug nuts before I elevated the car, but that manual was confusing. It didn't matter. Whatever I was doing was working, albeit extremely slowly.

Sweat bubbled from my scalp and ran down my face and into my eyes. I dabbed at my eyes with a fingertip until I remembered that I had no eye makeup on. Nothing was in danger of smearing. I was still getting used to the fact that I had given up all my female accoutrements. But when I finally realized that there was no mascara to sting my eyes, no carefully applied eyeliner to destroy, I wiped my hand across my face and into my eyes, smearing nothing but the dripping sweat.

I yanked at the tire, working it this way and that until it finally came off, a tangled, mangled, and extremely heavy loop of rubber that was filled with dirt, most of which ended up on me. I heaved it off to the side with a grunt, and this sound, this motion, transformed me. Instantly, both my body and my mind were possessed by some otherworldly masculine force. I had a new manly persona of sweat and filth. The testosterone churned through my veins. At any moment, my muscles might expand to split my shirt in several places, and my glistening, swollen torso would be revealed to every onlooker.

Adopting an apelike swagger, I lumbered back and forth along the side of the road, finally feeling confident that I might actually know what I was doing and that people passing by might think as much—"Why, look, Sam. There's a man who knows what he's doing." All I needed was a club and a dinosaur and I could kill dinner. The spare tire was merely an inflatable plastic inner tube in my hands. I ignored the fact that it was naturally much smaller and lighter than the original—it was me, not the tire, that was different.

It was on the car in no time, and I followed my innate masculine intuition, which told me to lower the car *before* I attempted to tighten the lug nuts. It all came so much more easily now, and when it was finished, I smacked my greasy black palms together, made a long, manly swipe across my forehead with the back of my hand, and stood back to admire my accomplishment. I was soaked, stinking, filthy, and at least thirty minutes had gone by—but I had changed my tire. It was like some strange rite of passage, and I felt proud.

When I arrived at work, I casually relayed my experience as if such things happened every day, making sure that everyone within earshot knew that I had been in full control at all times. But the novelty soon wore off. When the women at work heard of my feat, I was called on regularly to change the flat tires that sometimes happened in the parking lot. It was also assumed that I knew why cars wouldn't start, and that I would be able to fix them. It turned out that jumper cables were as much an accessory of manhood as my dangling earrings had been of womanhood. And I somehow gained the status of carnival strong man, being summoned to move heavy objects—file cabinets and tables in the meeting rooms —although my arm muscles were particularly pathetic. Suddenly I was expected to reach things in high places, although I hadn't grown an inch. I was expected, in other words, to be a man.

As far as my coworkers were concerned, I wasn't "passing," either. I just was, and I instantly became quite a convenience. For a time, it was flattering, and I was perfectly willing to fall into this role with my coworkers and friends. It gave me some definition and helped me outline my responsibilities. But I wasn't aware that I was gradually being inducted into a secret society—one in which I eventually came to realize that I didn't really belong.

THE SECRET MEN'S CLUB

Men have a secret club. I don't know how they manage to initiate everyone—it's got to be some code on the XY chromosome that's receptive to satellite beams or something, and the information is transferred that way. The thing about the secret men's club is that those who are already members—all male-born men—assume that everyone who looks like them is a member, too. There's no special handshake or cryptic password—unless it's "How 'bout them Broncos?" No, it's just naturally understood that if you look a certain way, you're automatically a member, you know the language, and you fit right in. I found out the hard way.

"So what's going on here?"

The man had plopped himself down next to me on the concrete bleachers that ran in an arc around the front of the outdoor stage. Below us was a large open area for people to dance or just to stand and watch the performance. It was the People's Fair, an outdoor festival in Denver that features row upon row of booths displaying arts and crafts, with dozens of food and beer vendors and several stages throughout Civic Center Park that showcase a variety of local entertainment. Although I attended the festival every year, it was my first time there as a man. My voice hadn't finished changing and I still had a cherubic innocence about my face. I wasn't certain whether this man had approached me to make a friend or to make a date. And if he wanted a date, I wasn't sure what gender he thought that date should be.

"It's a drag show," I said.

The drag show was an annual event and always brought a swarm of gay men to the stage to watch. He might have been one of them. Slender, with thick, dark hair and tanned skin, he was hardworking-man attractive and seemed pleasant enough, but I felt a stab of fear because I wasn't yet sure what my role was in this interaction.

"What's a drag show?" he asked.

Okay, he wasn't gay. That helped to clarify things a little. I explained to him the premise of a drag show, which he seemed to find hilarious.

"You're kidding. Men dressed up like women?" He roared, then nudged me with his elbow. "Well, hey. I can tell that's not a man down there."

He pointed with his head toward a woman below us in a scoop-necked halter top and cutoff shorts. Her breasts fell forward as she leaned over to talk to her friend, creating a dark line of cleavage down the center of her chest.

"Huh? Huh?" he said, continuing to jab his elbow into my arm. "I'd sure like to show her something. Wouldn't you?"

Then I knew what he thought I was—one of him, one of the members of the secret club that I was only beginning to learn about. He proceeded to point out the sexual merits or demerits of every woman in front of us, all the while jabbing at me as if to encourage my participation, while I sat, slightly numb, dumb-founded, and surprisingly conflicted. I was one of the guys and this was all the proof I needed. If he had been a grocery clerk, he would have "sirred" me with no question. My transition was already suc-cessful. This was a milestone that I should have been celebrating. I should have been feeling great, eager to rush home and e-mail all my friends. But I wasn't feeling great. In fact, I was feeling pretty awful. I was closer than I thought to being where he was, to being a comrade, a true member of the club. And this was part of the initiation. Why wasn't I excited?

But then the conflict—if I had been walking down there, only a year before, if I had been leaning over in a halter top or breezing by in my cutoff shorts, he would have been nudging someone else and saying the same things about me. He elbowed me again and I looked over at him, suddenly seeing a hulking, drooling Neanderthal, realizing that my silence signaled approval of, and maybe even agreement with, what he was saying. I knew what I should do and I knew what I should say. But I didn't.

I didn't because this was what I had wanted and this was where I had wanted to be. I had sacrificed a lot to become a member of this club, and it would be far too painful now to acknowledge that I didn't like the rules. And one of the rules, apparently, was that you could say pretty much whatever you wanted to say, as long as you were male and the person you were talking to was also male.

It took a long time to get over the guilt I felt when I left the drag show that day. I hadn't stuck up for my own kind, or at least my own former kind. I hadn't challenged the misogynistic notions of one sexist asshole. Because I was like him now—we were the same species. And this was what I had signed on for. Even though I told myself that he was only one man, that I knew plenty of guys who weren't like him in any way, the experience still weighed heavy, and I was reminded of it again a few days later when I called my mechanic to check on the progress of my tune-up. We talked for a minute and then he interrupted me.

"Listen, buddy," he said, his voice taking a sudden detour into panic mode. "I gotta call you back. I had Chinese for lunch and it's going straight through me. I gotta get to the can."

I tried to sound understanding and hang up as quickly as possible. I realized again that I was in the club. He would never have said that to me when I was female. This was, apparently, the stuff of male discussion—not just bodies but bodily functions, too, things that women don't discuss with their doctors, let alone a perfect stranger. At least I was starting to accumulate a series of role models who were showing me what I did *not* want to be. I continued to watch and listen, making new discoveries.

Another club rule turned out to be that other men don't care how apologetic you are when you accidentally pull in front of them on the road. They will flip you off and shout obscenities, even if you smile and shrug your shoulders and try to be polite about your mistake. If they happen to have a gun in the car, they will likely shoot you. Luckily, I never got shot at, but I learned to look forward at stoplights instead of glancing right or left to see who was beside me, because the wrong look might be taken as a challenge. I had never been taught to fight and knew that I would surely die in the effort.

An obscure club rule turned out to be that men rarely remark on the cuteness of a woman's child, and if they do so, it's at their own peril. The woman at the mall lugging an infant the size of a small load of laundry seemed grateful when I opened the door for her, but moved away quickly when I said, "Ooooh, what a cuuute beebee," in a cooing speech pattern apparently reserved for women only. Luckily, she didn't report me to the authorities—or maybe I just left the mall before they could catch up to me.

I was truly in a foreign land, fumbling around like a tourist who didn't know the customs or the language. But the problem was that I wasn't a tourist—I had moved there. And so much of the landscape was not only unfamiliar, it was unpleasant as well. A smile, an apology, even politeness—these things were often taken for weaknesses. Everything that I had learned in my forty-two years on earth proved pretty worthless in trying to adapt to this new and treacherous terrain. And then I realized that I wasn't sure I wanted to adapt. I remembered something else that my therapist had said —"The kind of man you are is the kind of man you are." Maybe I didn't have to be like them at all.

+ + +

There was a lot of my female self that I hadn't yet left behind, and the further I advanced into male territory, the more I found myself being pulled back to the center by the things I simply did not want to give up. I was doing things, thinking things, behaving in ways that our bi-gendered culture doesn't view as particularly male. Because of my socialization, I'd gone into the whole affair believing that men do certain things and women do others. Men are expected to be brave, strong, aggressive, protective, and to eschew emotion in favor of logic. Women are the soft ones, the polite ones, the emotional and caring ones.

I had bought into all these externally imposed expectations, and unfortunately, so do many other transmen. We reject all things "feminine" before, during, and after transition. We retrain ourselves to sit, walk, talk, and act in specific ways that are deemed "masculine" by a society that is hell-bent on preventing any variance in the gender roles that were set up specifically for the purpose of maintaining the status quo.

But I had to admit that I liked some of the female parts of myself. I didn't necessarily want to stop being emotional. I was proud of my compassion and empathy. I liked that I cared about the world, that I loved little puppies, that I wanted fresh flowers in my house, and that I thought it was okay to cry. Spiders still terrified me, and I couldn't have cared less which teams were in the Final Four basketball playoffs. But somewhere along the way, I had developed the idea that all of that was wrong. I, like transmen everywhere, and like *men* everywhere, had been brainwashed, and it was so internalized that I didn't realize that we were being controlled by a force other than ourselves. How were we, as transmen, supposed to establish our own identities, be our own men, when we were allowing society's definitions of maleness to control our actions and behaviors?

It was time for me to start listening to my own (increasingly deep) voice. Transsexual people, I realized, could be the ones to bring down the gender barriers that had been established in our world. We were not only changing ourselves, we were changing society. We were changing culture. We were, and are, a new breed, people who can do whatever we damn well please and act in any manner that defines us as people, whether that be playing tackle football or attending a Broadway musical. There were no barriers, there were no boundaries—or if there were, we had allowed society to set them up for us. And we could decide to tear them down.

I don't profess to be a man now, except when forced to make a choice on some form that doesn't recognize alternative states of being. But the fact that the world sees me as completely male doesn't mean I'm tricking anyone. I'm just me. I've blended the female parts and the male parts of myself into a whole being. Granted, that being appears male, but that was my choice for the outside and is not *entirely* reflective of what's going on underneath.

Our society tends to put very finite expectations on male and female thought and behavior and has ways to punish those who don't conform. Although I continue to struggle with the rigid boundaries that the culture has put on someone who looks male, like I do, I have found freedom in incorporating the male and female pieces that were already there and not allowing myself to be bound by others' expectations of manhood. In other words, I don't have to wear a tie and I have a good excuse.

Part of the transition process is discovering how much blending of masculine and feminine is comfortable. Many transpeople tend to go overboard at first, moving to the far reaches of masculinity (or femininity), becoming more macho (or femme) than someone who has always lived in the gender. This has a lot to do with insecurity and attempting to find a place on the masculine/feminine continuum. Some transpeople find that place comfortable—this is where they have always lived, at least in their minds. But many eventually gravitate back toward center, where male and female characteristics, as defined by our culture, can both harmoniously inhabit one body. But the pressure to conform can be almost unbearable at times. I was on a gender seesaw for quite a while, and even today, I still have my ups and downs.

Although I struggled for an internal gender identity, going through phases of "real manhood" and "redefining manhood" and "incorporating the feminine into manhood," society does not allow for any ambiguous selections when it comes to gender. However, the bureaucracy must think that we're not always sure ourselves, which is why gender questions on forms usually come with multiple-choice answers, allowing for at least a 50 percent chance of getting it right. You can check "male" or you can check "female," but you never have the option of checking "all of the above" or "none of the above." I know several people who created their own selection for the census—sort of a "write-in gender"—but I was told that, in those cases, the census takers just guessed, usually by looking at the first name on the form. In the United States, as in most countries, you are your papers. Whatever your driver's license, birth certificate, and passport say determine whether you are called "sir" or "ma'am."

Each state has different laws and policies regarding gender reassignment and what makes a man a man, since state governments are not, unfortunately, as ethereal as my therapist was. In my state, there are no papers or court hearings that will legally change a person's gender—the closest I could come was changing the gender on my driver's license. First I changed my name, then I changed my driver's license. Then, no matter how insecure I was feeling about my acquired masculinity, I only had to look at my license, see the "M," and know how I was supposed to feel and behave. It's not so important to me anymore, but it means a lot to those people who control the paperwork. On this planet, knowing your own and someone else's gender is second in importance only to knowing which door leads to the men's room and which to the women's. So even if you see yourself in the middle somewhere, you still have to make up your mind—it goes with the paperwork.

It was easy to get my name changed. I went in, filled out a handful of forms, plunked down my hard-earned $44, went in front of a judge, and promised that I wasn't trying to escape my creditors (with all the money I owe, they'd find me anyway). I had written "gender reassignment" under "reason for name change" on my paperwork. The judge didn't question it. I walked out a few minutes later with an official order that stayed official as long as I published it for three consecutive weeks and sent proof to the court.

Next stop, the Department of Motor Vehicles. The young woman who assisted me didn't bat an eye when I showed her the required letter from my doctor and my court papers. She just said, "Oh, we'll have to change that F to an M," did so, and then said, "Step over there, Matthew, and get your picture taken." At the Social Security office, the woman examined my papers carefully, punched something into the computer, and said, "Okay, sir, your new card will be in the mail in about two weeks." Friendly, friendly people. Trans-friendly people. But it's easy to be trans friendly when the proof is right in front of you. No matter how sensitive these employees were, they were still thinking, as most of us do, in terms of two genders. And they had legal paperwork to tell them which one of the two I was.

But the "M" and "F" designations on driver's licenses and other forms can often get in the way of identifying people as who they really are. There are people who prefer not to define themselves by gender at all. It must be difficult for them to have to choose an "M" or an "F" when an "N" or even an "N/A" category might be more appropriate.

When I began identifying as transgendered, and later as transsexual, I became acutely aware of how important gender definitions are in our society. We truly do define ourselves by our genitals, then cover them up, as if they were our happy secrets. If we're going to identify ourselves by what's inside our pants, then let's at least display it so everyone can get a good look. And if we're more civilized than that, let's take into account all the gender-diverse people among us and make the world a more comfortable place for them as well.

Gender diversity is here and it's not going away. There are any number of ways it can be dealt with, but so far, I've liked Elyse's way the best—at least until it's no longer necessary to ask people what they are in order to address them. Many transpeople, maybe the majority, do eventually decide to become "completely male" or "completely female," and sometimes become stricter in their own gender roles and behaviors than many nontranspeople. Whatever works. But there's a growing number, like myself, who are willing and able to blend their gender characteristics into one big "What are you?" and live out perfectly normal and satisfactory lives.

I've been accused of wanting to do away with gender altogether. Those who hear my views sometimes come away with the idea that I would prefer one big blur of humanity, where people walk around with male and female sex organs or no sex organs at all or any combination of physical and psychological attributes that would prevent any kind of gender designation. Actually, there are plenty of people walking around right now who defy specific gender designation—they might be transsexual or intersexed or just plain rebellious—but they're out there every day and they're doing society no harm.

I don't support eliminating gender designations—I only support expanding them. Racial categories continue to increase and now far more adequately encompass the varied racial and ethnic identities of our modern world than did the three antiquated categories of my youth—Caucasoid, Negroid, and Mongoloid. I haven't seen these used for years and no one complains. Most young people have never even heard of these terms. Racial identity is far more complicated than this, and we are far more evolved in our thinking about it, although we still have quite a ways to go. That some people identify with more than one racial or ethnic designation is now commonplace. My fantasy is that, in the future, there will be several gender choices available, including the standard "male" and "female."

It's true that, simply by transitioning—injecting male hormones, undergoing chest reconstruction, taking a male name, and wearing men's clothing and a male haircut—I have bought into a large part of society's binary gender system. When I'm not being accused of trying to rid our culture of gender, I'm lambasted for reinforcing narrow gender stereotypes. For me, it's simply a matter of comfort with myself and with what I want to look like.

That many transpeople strictly adhere to gender stereotypes while others reject them has more to do with the identities that these people have forged for themselves before, during, and after transition than with any need to make a political or social statement. Just like everyone else, who we are is reflected, at least in part, in how we present ourselves. Like snowflakes and those questionable chicken nuggets, no two transpeople are alike. Each possesses a separate identity formed through an individual struggle with or against the tide, and whether that identity is male, female, some of both, or neither, it's definitely a part of the journey. Me, I'm a transman—until a better label comes along.

PART THREE

Trans Bodies

Hormones, Glorious Hormones

There's nothing like going through a second adolescence in middle age. Male puberty is a curious thing that's best undertaken by someone with a lot of youthful energy, exuberance, and resilience —someone, say, thirteen or fourteen years old. But if you missed it the first time around, intramuscular injections of pharmaceutical testosterone can re-create the experience so realistically that you can almost picture yourself in the middle school cafeteria preparing for a food fight.

The first testosterone shot is probably the most eagerly awaited moment in a transman's life and one that is never forgotten. Although nothing much happens afterward, you know that you have crossed the threshold into a new beginning. There's a myth that the shot produces some kind of "high," or that you instantly transform from mild-mannered reporter into superhero, giving the impression that all transmen are walking around in a drug-induced state of hypermasculinity. In fact, the hormone sits in the muscle and slowly disseminates into the bloodstream over the course of several days. There are definite highs and lows as testosterone levels wax and wane in the system, but the hormone affects everyone differently. Some guys claim to become lethargic or to feel out of sorts or "just not right" as the hormone dissipates and the time for another shot grows near. Others can forget their shot day (usually every two weeks) altogether unless they remember to mark their calendars. But it's not likely that a transman just beginning hormone therapy will lose track of the date for his next shot. Once the decision to transition is made, the changes can't happen fast enough.

I remember the day of my first shot—on Martin Luther King, Jr.'s birthday in 1998—when I sat in my therapist's waiting room, sacrificing my session to give her time to write the letter that doctors require in order to administer the hormones. With letter in hand, I telephoned my doctor's office with the news that I was officially qualified to begin hormone therapy. Although the receptionist was completely unmoved by this development in my life and tried to put me off until the next day, I pressed and pressed until she finally told me to come right over. I arrived breathless at the doctor's office and left twenty minutes later with a healthy dose of testosterone in my butt and the fantasy that I would wake up the next morning looking like Grizzly Adams. Unfortunately, it took several months for any hint of facial hair, but *something* grew within a matter of days. I remembered scoffing at a friend when he told me that his clitoris had grown almost immediately, but there I was in the shower, four days after my shot, when I happened upon something quite unfamiliar.

"What *is* that?" I asked out loud in my then-still-soprano female voice. When I realized that the small, swollen protuberance under my fingers was not a fast-growing tumor, I was jubilant. I waited eagerly to see how much more it would grow. I'm still waiting.

But like a young male on the brink of manhood, I was quickly distracted by other concerns. Overnight, my sex drive rocketed through the roof. I think that, by now, it's sailing somewhere over Cleveland. I rapidly developed a new hobby and understood why unenlightened mothers warn their sons to keep their hands outside the covers. I also had a newfound understanding of the eighth grade boys I used to teach. They were restless and inattentive, and

I often wondered if they'd been fathered by space aliens. Now I knew their dilemma, and if I ever return to teaching, I'll be much more sympathetic. In fact, it would probably behoove all middle school teachers, both male and female, to try a few shots of testosterone before their first teaching assignment—the women, so they could understand, and the men, so they could remember.

Between the sexual fantasies, the activity that quelled them, and running to the mirror every five minutes to see if hair had sprouted anywhere, there was little time for much else. I did manage to hold down a job, do some writing, and engage in occasional social activities, but the excitement of a newly hormoned body continued, and I was certain that, any day, I would develop the manly appearance of which I had dreamed. Testosterone does miraculous things, but I soon learned that it has its limitations: it can only act on what genetics have already programmed. Therefore, guys who disdain the hirsute can end up suffering hairy backs and shoulders, while guys like me, who covet body hair of any kind, can turn out disappointingly smooth. Guys who wish for a head of hair akin to Elvis Presley can wind up bald, while those of us with thick, unruly mops never get the thinning hair we long for.

Just like our nontrans counterparts, we can only look to our relatives to determine what will happen to us. Since my own father was a hairless wonder everywhere but on top of his head, I believe now that my fate has been decided. No amount of male hormone will give me the wooly chest that I desire. But at least my chest is as close to a male one as the miracles (and expense) of surgery will allow. And that has become good enough for me.

FLAT BUSTED

Chest reconstruction is often the second major step in a female-to-male transition and it's a welcome subtraction to the household. One of the problems with transition, as in furnishing a home, is that you think you'll be satisfied once you get that male haircut / choose a new name / change your driver's license / start hormones, but each progression only leaves you longing for more. The new couch would look so much better with matching end tables and the new body would look so much better without them. Chest, or "top," surgery is one of the most fulfilling accomplishments of transition. You can finally abandon painful and artery-constricting binders. You can wear the flimsiest of T-shirts with no telltale binder or bra lines. You can even take your shirt off in public.

There are many doctors in North America and abroad who perform this surgery, with costs averaging anywhere from \$3,500 to \$7,500. I chose a surgeon in San Francisco, one of my favorite cities, where I had high hopes of combining business and pleasure—but sightseeing with drainage tubes snaking loosely down both sides of my body proved less than ideal. Even so, the real attraction was the masculine chest that I would sport as soon as the bandages came off.

Breasts are a significant identifier of females in our culture and, therefore, something that transmen usually want to get rid of as soon as possible. For me, the "ma'ams" virtually disappeared after the surgery, even though my face was still the same for quite a while. Breasts are one of the strongest signifiers of gender, stronger even than genitalia, since they are visible to everyone, even through clothing. But it wasn't until after my surgery that I realized the insanity of our culture's insistence on sexualizing the female breast.

In the park, in broad daylight, with the same basic genitalia that I had possessed since the nurse wrote "Female" on my birth certificate, I could shed my shirt without any fear of being arrested or (unfortunately) even ogled. A few short months earlier, I could never have done such a thing. What was the difference?

I knew that female breasts were somehow a sexual thing long before mine actually were. Even on the beach as a child, I had to keep my nondescript chest covered at all times. And when I finally developed breasts in adolescence, I soon learned that what I had wasn't enough when the boys flocked to my more amply endowed best friend. I always felt inadequate as a female—I never felt "female" enough—and somehow I came to the misguided conclusion that it was because my breasts weren't big enough. For whatever Freudian reason, I equated breast size with womanliness, and I eventually decided that the only remedy was to get implants. So, at age thirty, I did.

They helped for a while. I got at least twice the male attention that I had gotten pre-D cup. It pleased me and it bothered me. Even as my boyfriends delighted in my chest, I questioned them as to their obsession. "Breasts are just fat tissue and milk ducts," I insisted (leaving out the silicone part). "What's so great about that?" They couldn't answer me rationally. They were operating under the influence of testosterone, and now, with more firsthand understanding, I'm able to forgive them.

It wasn't difficult to give up my breasts, even though I had spent a fortune on them. The whole point, after all, was to get rid of the markers of womanhood, and after the implants, they were pretty big markers. But even though I thought I understood the sexual significance of breasts in our culture, I had no idea how far it really went until mine were gone.

When my fellow FtMs asked to see my chest shortly after the surgery, it took me a minute to realize that I wasn't going to be flashing them. Nontransmale friends I didn't know intimately asked to touch it, then ran their hands across it with awe. I silently adjusted to the fact that they weren't copping a feel. Even now, whenever I walk around my apartment shirtless, I sometimes worry about exposing myself to the neighbors. I could walk down the street without a shirt and the only thing they could arrest me for is scaring little children. I couldn't be arrested for indecent exposure. My chest isn't sexual anymore.

The surgery involved a double mastectomy with some minor sculpting, smaller nipples that resulted from the surgeon taking one nipple and making it into two, and pink, angry scars that ran across my torso just above my diaphragm, as if I'd gotten into a fight with Zorro and lost. The first time I put on a tight T-shirt and walked out of my house, it was all worth it. But the true test was taking that T-shirt off.

I had cased out the park beforehand. It was several miles from my house and it always seemed strangely deserted on weekends. But even so, I chose a spot that was as far as possible from the empty picnic tables, the unused playground equipment, and the vacant soccer field. I sat in my car for a few minutes, terribly afraid and trying to convince myself that nontransmen did this all the time, even though most of them have never learned what I consider to be a valuable lesson: just because you *can* take off your shirt, that doesn't mean you *should*. But I wanted to get a little tan, and I wanted the experience of actually taking off my shirt in a public place—with as few members of the public present as possible.

I finally got out and edged through the trees and down the grassy slope to a clearing where I could be in the sun. Then I arranged my towel on the grass. It had to be this way. No, it had to be that way. The corners had to line up. The angle had to be toward the sun, but the edges couldn't be in the shade. It couldn't be on that prickly dandelion or near that dog poop. When it had finally been configured in every way possible, when it finally seemed just right and I had no more excuse to mess with it, I looked around. There was no one to be seen. There was no one to see me.

I sat down and pulled tenderly on the Velcro of my sandals. It was important that it be separated just so. Eventually, there was no more Velcro to pull at. I slipped my sandals off my feet and set them aside on the grass, lining them up carefully, toe matching toe and heel matching heel. Then I looked around. I had to have a drink of water, and I dug in my bag for the bottle. I had to apply sunscreen to my lips or they would burn. The towel that was to go under my head had to be carefully folded. Then I had to look around again. Did I have my car keys or had they somehow gotten lost in the treacherous descent down the little slope? No, they were still there. I looked around. There was nothing left to do. The shirt had to come off.

I grabbed the hem of my T-shirt and yanked it fiercely upward, as if it were on fire, then I threw it down next to me and heaved my upper body backward. I was lying down. In the sun. In public. With no shirt. I was naked. And even if people came along, they wouldn't care. Even if they bothered to look, the most that they would see would be the scars, and they might think, "Oh, that poor man, I wonder what happened to him," but that would be the extent of it. It took me a while to convince myself of that as I lay rigid, my muscles tight, my jaw clenched, ferociously determined in my nudity. But the longer I lay there without reprisal, the sun beating down on my naked, scarred torso, the more I started to relax.

I had almost begun to drift off when the revelation formed in my head: all the push-up bras, all the tight T-shirts, all the low-cut sweaters—none of that existed anymore. None of it ever would again. I could do this anytime I wanted. It was legal now. It was decent now. Even with the same genitalia that I had carried around with me since birth, I could now take off my shirt in the middle of the day, in the middle of a public park, and nothing, absolutely nothing, would happen. My chest was asexual.

I wondered what would happen if a woman with a double mastectomy, an obvious woman who bore the female gender markers of our culture, decided to take her shirt off and lay out in a public park. Would she be arrested or ignored? With the emphasis that we place on breasts, either outcome would seem an insult. The longer I remained topless, stretched out on my towel, the more I questioned the sanity of our society's overblown obsession with two hunks of flesh. And, even more, I marveled at how easily I had become desexualized by the lack of them.

My mother had died of complications from breast cancer after the removal of a single breast, and my biggest fear as a woman was that I might follow in her footsteps, losing the one thing that I believed made me female. Now the whole thing seemed ridiculous. Lying there with my female genitalia and my male chest, I could see the whole breast thing for what it really was—absurd.

I've recovered from feeling naked every time I take off my shirt. The surgical scars are still there and will always be with me (and quite visible, since my chest is still as smooth as Humphrey Bogart was in *Casablanca*). I've gotten used to them—I rarely notice them anymore, although I'm sure others do. The thing that keeps me shirted now, even on the hottest of days, is the lovely little beer gut that I developed when my body fat redistributed, an unfair consequence for someone who doesn't even imbibe. Men carry their body fat around their middles like an inner tube being hauled to a swimming hole. While I used to protest, as a female, that all those photographs of beautiful women in girlie magazines were obviously airbrushed, I say the same thing now about the models in men's fitness magazines. I'm sure that nobody really looks like that. The shirtless guys at the local park playing volley-ball? They must have their own private airbrushers following them around.

The reality is that I don't have a perfect body. But I never did. And most people don't. So the other reality is that I'm pretty much like everybody else—at least with my clothes on.

DICKLESS in Denver

When you have a transsexual body, you had better get used to being less than the perfect specimen that's touted in the popular media. Female-to-male headaches include being shorter than the average guy, having wider hips (we were originally made for childbirth, and testosterone, as powerful as it is, does nothing to change the bone structure), sporting permanent chest scars, and usually navigating a man's world without the one thing that society says all men must possess—no, not a fire engine red Corvette. Take another guess.

Penises are a very big deal (or a very little deal, depending on how you look at it) in the transmale community. Testosterone makes the clitoris grow, but usually only enough to be visible to the naked eye. Some guys have better luck than others, depending on genetics, but this is one thing you will never ask your father about, so you just have to wait and see. The question "Dad, how big is your dick?" is simply not uttered in polite families. But once hormones take hold, you wish that you knew so you would have some idea of where you were headed. The competition among transmen is fierce. Bragging about two inches, unheard of in nontransmale society, is often standard fare at nouveau transman get-togethers. And those lucky enough to be able to afford phalloplastic surgery are definitely at the top of the food chain.

For those of us whose goals (and incomes) are more modest,

there exists an array of prosthetics that can give the impression of a living organ inside tight jeans. My first pants stuffer cost around $100, and although it was unattractive and a little complicated to wear, I felt good when I had it on. It was nothing more than a band of elastic that circled my hips and attached to a rather stiff, tan-colored tube made from some unidentifiable material, with imitation testicles hanging beneath it that were stuffed with small granules and covered tightly with a piece cut from a pair of pantyhose. But when I put it on, something changed. When I looked in the mirror, there was a bulge in my pants, just underneath and to the left of the zipper. There was substance in my pants that I could feel. And when I went out into the world, whether anyone looked at my crotch or not, I knew what was there—the mark of my manhood. Like the silicone breasts of my past, this was a visible sign, to myself and to the world, of what I was.

After a while, though, the excitement of having dangling bulk between my legs turned to tedium—it was always so *there*.

"Do guys know that they have a dick and balls? I mean, can you feel yours all the time?" I asked my friend Keith.

As odd as it might seem to others, this question didn't surprise him. Keith was one of my few male friends who seemed to delight in helping me acclimate to my new maleness. No question was too personal for him. He knew everything about my body, so it was only fair that I knew whatever I wanted to know about his.

"Yeah, I pretty much know they're there all the time," he said, leaning back and putting his hands behind his head like a wise sage leading a novice toward enlightenment. "Sometimes I'm more aware of my dick, like certain times during the day when it's more tumescent."

Tumescent. Now there was a word. With multiple washings, my pants stuffer became tumescent as well. The problem was that it never became untumescent. It just got stiffer and stiffer over time until I finally either had to abandon it or walk around looking perpetually aroused. But I got quite a lot of use out of it before it hardened itself out of existence. My friend Marty wasn't so lucky, as his penis and balls were destroyed when his dog got hold of the contraption and paraded it through the house, clutching it in his teeth like a dead rat, then using it as a favorite chew toy until it was shredded.

I later moved on to a more pliable, natural variety that I could drop in my pants at a moment's notice. The problem was that it tended to drop out at a moment's notice as well—usually on the floor of the men's room when I lowered my pants to pee. There are several men walking around now, those who happened to be in the stalls next to me when such a thing occurred, who are terrified to go into certain bathrooms for fear that they might lose the best parts of themselves. So sorry—my mother told me never to sit on a public toilet seat.

But no matter what stuffer I was using, it always came off at night. It always came off before I took a shower. My manhood wasn't permanent. It was only an illusion. All I had to do was look down to remember that I wasn't quite whole. I could have invested $300 or so for a realistically shaped and molded penis and balls, one fashioned with veins and a carefully shaped head, all in a shade to match my own skin tone. This penis glued on with special medical glue and stayed on for several days, even in the shower. I could have shaved my pubic hair and glued on this penis, and for a while, it seemed like a good idea if I could come up with the money. But it wouldn't have been any more real than the floppy, peach-toned stuffer that I was already using. Was this what it meant to be a man?

I wore some type of pants stuffer for over two years. It didn't take me nearly that long to figure out that other people weren't thinking about my crotch. It just took me that long to stop thinking about it myself. When I finally decided to fully accept myself as transsexual, instead of male, I was able to ease into a stuffer-less state and go absolutely anywhere without a bulge in my pants. Somehow, I've survived.

But many transguys simply don't feel complete without the "real thing"—a surgically constructed and attached penis. And if find-ing a partner is a goal, the missing link becomes even more im-portant. It seems to be a little easier for transmen who desire female partners—many women don't rank a penis at the top of their list of necessary attributes in a man. For transmen who are attracted to men, and thus considered "gay" because of their male appearance, it can be more difficult. And, as luck would have it (my luck, at least), I am one of those guys.

I even made up my own joke when I first started my transition:
Question: What do you call a gay man without a penis?
Answer: Single.

I was prepared for this reality before I even began my transi-tion. Knowing my own fondness for this spirited male organ, and having some familiarity with the gay personals, I had an idea that sex and romance would not be forthcoming for a nouveau-gay transman. My gay male friends were discouraged for me and some even questioned why I would make such a transition when I was getting plenty of sex as a female. That was an easy one to answer, since most of us spend more than 90 percent of our lives *not* hav-ing sex. That 90 percent should at least be enjoyed in the correct gender. They were still concerned that I wouldn't get laid, but nei-ther did anyone offer himself up for the cause. No, I was on my own for this one.

Luckily, I had an acquaintance who was well versed in cruising for sex. He explained to me that I was lucky because I had small earlobes and small thumbs. Apparently, at least in his circles, men examined thumbs and earlobes to determine dick size. My luck, then, stemmed from the fact that if a man saw my hideously shrunken thumbs and earlobes and was still interested in me, penis size didn't matter to him. It made me self-conscious, but it allowed me to blame my early rejections on the fact that I wore earmuffs and mittens to the bars in the middle of the summer. I considered surgery, but decided that, for the money I'd spend, I could just hire one of those cute male escorts for twenty years. Celibacy even crossed my mind—that is, until my next testosterone shot.

But all that was early on in my transition, before I realized that there are worse things than being dickless in Denver. My genitalia has served me well for more years than I care to discuss, and will continue to do so—and did I mention multiple orgasms? It's not an idea to scoff at when you're mainlining male hormones in middle age. And anyway, my own imagined inadequacy is probably nothing when compared to a male-born gay man who doesn't quite measure up. I wonder about those men who have teeny weenies, who are impotent, paralyzed, or in some other way don't possess the "let me worship your package" accoutrements that seem to be standard fare for the community as portrayed in the gay media and in gay porn.

Since starting hormones, I understand the phrase "thinking with your little head." But what if it really is a little head? What if it doesn't function the way it should? If sex is only about a big, hard penis and seven inches is a little on the small side, what happens to everyone else? I've seen my share (and several other people's) of dicks in my lifetime and I know how much they vary in size, shape, and capacity.

For me, the image of myself as a transman instead of a "man" has served me well in this area. For nontransmen who have focused all their lives on the penis as some elongated badge of their masculinity, any minor mishap can turn into a major threat to manhood. I don't have to worry about that threat. I didn't put my power into an appendage to begin with. But it's true that suddenly "becoming gay" did make me feel a little, well, "little" for a while.

Although I didn't transition to become a gay man, I knew that I would be perceived as such and that any potential partners would, at the very least, have to find male attributes attractive—but not all of them, only the ones that I possessed. My first rejection was the hardest—or should I say the most difficult? There was a blissfully ignorant period in the initial stages of my transition when I somehow believed that my lack of a penis wouldn't matter *that* much. I was a nice guy with an interesting life and a good sense of humor and people on the street didn't run screaming when they looked at me. How important could a penis be? I got my answer and it wasn't the one I wanted.

Online romance was something that I had scoffed at for years. Even though a female friend of mine had fallen in love that way, and eventually married the guy, I knew that there were more hucksters and frauds out there than truly honorable people. And I, of course, was one of the truly honorable ones.

After I put my profile online as a gay man, I got my share of instant messages from men claiming to be doing things to themselves that it would have been physically impossible to do while typing words on a keyboard. All the same, I sometimes went along with it, more out of boredom than an actual desire for sex with a computer. But true to my female nature, the guy who really caught my interest was the one who was actually interested in me.

"What do you like to do? What are your hobbies? What do you do for a living?"

He typed in real questions and never once mentioned that he might be, or that he wanted to be, doing anything complicated to himself in front of an inert screen. I was hooked, and I told him all about myself—except for one very small detail.

We finally decided to meet, and I figured I would tell him then. I wanted him to *know* me first, I wanted him to *like me for me*— I could practically hear the falsetto female voice inside me. And then that same voice said, *You're a fraud.*

I hadn't exactly lied to him, but I certainly hadn't been honest. I was a man, right? I was a gay man, right? Not really. At least not in the way that I had led him to believe. And the unfortunate truth was that I was not a man or a gay man in the way that I had led myself to believe, either. I really was kidding myself this time. I'd known other gay female-to-males who were living as gay men and were succeeding at it quite well. But not only wasn't I succeeding, I wasn't even certain that I wanted to succeed.

My identity was still a mystery to me, but I knew one thing for certain. In this situation, *I* was the Internet huckster. I was the one misrepresenting myself. It might have been unintentional, but it was true. And even though I had wanted to meet him, to have him like me for me, there was no way that he was going to like someone who was misleading him. The next time we "talked," I told him.

"I'm a female-to-male transsexual," I typed into the Instant Message.

There was a pause, followed by the message, "Does that mean your equipment doesn't work?"

"No. It means I have no equipment."

Another pause. "I wish you would have told me sooner."

"So do I."

"But I really like penises."

Of course you do.

And that was the beginning of the end of my first and only Internet romance. And it was the beginning of my decision to be open about my transsexuality to every potential romantic and sexual partner that I met. Which was the beginning of the end of my love life.

I had other opportunities, but they strayed even further from the *like me for me* edict that was obviously going to be necessary and even further into the *penis as required equipment* category. Being so inexperienced in the realm of anonymous sex, it took me several minutes to realize that the man who was displaying himself to me on a darkened street wasn't a flasher. Of course, I had nothing to display in return. In the local cruising park, when I nodded at a man who was sitting on a bench, I meant the gesture as "Hello." He understood it as "Let's go" and headed for the nearest clump of trees, turning to see if I was following him. When I realized what I had set in motion, I disappeared faster than day-old doughnuts at my office. He would have been mightily disappointed with sex that was so anonymous that I wouldn't even unzip my pants. But I learned that, at least in that particular park, a kiss might still be a kiss, but a nod isn't always just a nod.

Coming out isn't just for gay people. As a transsexual, I had to come out *to* gay people. And any men who had shown an interest before my announcement vanished like quarters in a slot machine when they heard the news.

Certainly, there were days when I felt that Mother Nature was nothing but a cruel practical jokester—right up there with Father Time. Talk about abusive parents. But in the days that followed my rejection, after berating myself as a man and pummeling myself with the idea that I would never be adequate, I came to a realization.

If I had been born male, I might have been happily involved with the man of my dreams instead of sitting around sulking and feeling sorry for myself. But if I had been born male, would I have appreciated it with anywhere near the intensity that I appreciated what I was? Would I find joy in even the smallest changes in my body and in my world? Would I wake up each day like a little kid, eager to see what new discoveries and excitements that day would bring? And I knew that, if I had been born male, I would never have had the unique opportunity to see the world from both sides, to experience both the female and the male aspects of life.

What a gift that was—one that I never would have received if things hadn't happened exactly the way that they did. I didn't want to give it up—not for all the sex in the world. Not even for the perfect relationship. And I decided then that I needed to be thankful for the gift that I had been given—the chance to love each day of my life because I was better able to appreciate what I had, where I'd been, and who I was becoming.

I went through a lot of rationalization at first about not having a penis. It would have been nice to have something in my jeans that didn't drop out after I had dropped it in. It still would be. But I've learned to be comfortable with what I have (or don't have) and have managed to lead a fairly ordinary, yet fulfilling, life. As long as I keep my clothes on, I'm a relatively unremarkable middle-aged guy. Underneath, I possess a trans body, which would be my legacy whether or not it had a surgically attached penis. And underneath that trans body, there's a whole lot more.

THE BODY PUBLIC

Transsexuals have transsexual bodies, no matter how skilled our surgeons. And in a society that values physical beauty and physical perfection, we're often left behind. As a female, I was bombarded with images of what I was supposed to look like and how much money I was supposed to spend to get that look. Most "fashion" magazines geared to women are primarily pages of advertisements, informing women, with glossy, colorful photographs and text, about what they must purchase in order to look like the women in the ads. Although the ideal female form changes based on what society needs from its women at any given time, it's still highly structured and generally unattainable by the majority. In recent years, eating disorders among women have increased dramatically and elementary school girls report that they are dieting. Our culture's expectations of its women can be unmerciful.

But what about the men? Men in our society have historically been immune to the destructive images presented as attractive. It's only been recently that researchers have identified eating disorders in men, that men have begun to seek out cosmetic surgery, and that an ideal body type has become specified for men and flaunted in the gay and straight media. The slender, muscular, well-defined, and eternally young physique is now de rigueur for men. For today's studly guys, small butts, narrow hips, shapely pectorals, and six-pack abs are almost more important than a six-figure annual income.

The media, driven by advertising revenues, decide on the ideal, creating an image that is just beyond our grasp, but one that can surely be achieved if we drive the right car, wear the right clothes, choose the right makeup, or buy the right magazine. With all the emphasis on the perfect body, where does this leave transmen? How do our bodies fit?

It's true that testosterone does redistribute fat and put on muscle, but we are never going to completely lose that butt and those hips. Hormones don't act on bone structure. And although a few guys have told me that they have actually lost weight on T, it tends to pack on the pounds and bloat us like the Hindenburg. That sexy bulge in our pants comes off at night along with our boxers—at least for most of us. And I have yet to see an underwear model with surgical scar lines along his chest.

Where this does leave transmen is either behind closed doors, covered by bulky sweaters in the middle of summer, or totally redefining our sense of an acceptable male body. We can't look to the media to portray us or support us. We can't look to male-born men to model appropriate bodies for us. We can look only to ourselves and begin to construct our own male body image from the transsexual bodies that we have. Countless transmen have done it, choosing many different body types to display proudly, whether they be muscular, large, thin, hairy, scarred, tattooed, pierced, or whatever else fits an individual's best personal image. The problem with the media is that we never see the infinite variety of great bodies out there—the ones that are special, the ones that reflect the infinite variety of our world.

Becoming comfortable with a trans body is a long and arduous process with a goal that many never achieve. To think of oneself as a man can sometimes make the process more difficult. To think of oneself as a transman, which might not be the ideal for many guys, at least allows for variations in the body that aren't seen in media depictions of the male. Everyone's body is unique. The narrow images presented to us do not represent the majority of people, trans or not, who are born every day and live perfectly happy and normal lives. As transmen, we simply take our uniqueness a step further. My body works and I'm lucky to have it. Do I want a penis, an unscarred chest, small hips, and the perfect butt? I wouldn't turn it all down if it were offered, but it would also take away a part of me—that part that says I'm unique.

Talking about my body has become as normal for me as discussing what I had for breakfast. As a transsexual, my body has, in many ways, become less my property. Speaking and writing about it contribute to that, but with the books available that chronicle various surgeries, with the television talk shows that highlight—and sometimes exploit—transsexual people, and with all the information only a few clicks away on the Internet, my body almost seems to be in the public domain—which means that I had better like it myself, even if no one else does.

It took me a while to get used to my body at all and even longer to accept it. I finally decided to force the issue, to face myself—my whole self. I came home one day, stripped off my clothes, and glared at myself in the mirror. The experience wasn't exactly comforting, but it was real. It was me.

"I'm a transsexual man," I said to myself. "This is what a transsexual man's face looks like."

What a transsexual man's face looked like, at least in my case, was round and immature, the face of someone on the downside of puberty—with patchy facial hair, a small nose, soft skin—but yet someone strangely old, with a creased forehead, crow's-feet, puffy pockets under the eyes. A middle-aged woman, a teenaged boy—a middle-aged, teenaged boy. Even now, I sometimes don't recognize that face. But it's mine.

"This is what a transsexual man's body looks like," I told myself.

What a transsexual man's body looked like, at least in my case, was round and slightly undefined—struggling chest and arm muscles, with rounded biceps and shoulders, but with thin, almost invisible veins in place of the pronounced and snakelike arm veins of a male-born man. Visible pink-white scars across the chest with small nipples sitting high above them and then a straight-up-and-down torso with no waist, but with hips that still flared from a widened pelvic structure that would never go away.

Although I hadn't shaved my legs for a couple of years by that time, the hair that had grown in was long and sparse, beginning just above the knee and trickling downward. For some unexplained reason, the leg hair that had caused me so much embarrassment in my preadolescence, when my mother had refused to let me shave, didn't come back when I needed it most. But in the middle of all that, in between the legs and the torso, there was nothing. Nothing but a thatch of hair that had started to grow slowly up my abdomen and down the center of my thighs. This was not a man's body. But this was a transsexual man's body. And it was—and is—my body. Forever.

The majority of people never see my naked body, where all the clues to my transness lie. This is good for me and, no doubt, a special relief for the majority of people. Once testosterone wormed its way into my cells for good, I began to look just like every other average Joe on the street—and, believe me, there are far more average Joes than there are guys who look like they just walked off a magazine page. Once I became comfortable with just being trans, the comfort with my body followed. But it was sometimes difficult to find that comfort under the scrutiny of friends and coworkers who seemed even more fascinated with my changing self than I was.

In the past, professionals recommended getting away from the familiar, moving to a new town, and starting all over after transition as an entirely new person. This advice is now seen by many as old-fashioned, and an increasing number of people are choosing to remain in their towns, neighborhoods, and jobs during and after transition. But transitioning in front of an audience can have its drawbacks.

After they got over their initial shock, my friends and coworkers took an almost voyeuristic delight in watching what they called my "transformation."

"Have you grown taller?" *No. The ends of my bones fused in adolescence, which was thirty-some years ago.*

"Do you think it was your sex change that made you sick this year?" *No, my "sex change" didn't make me sick. I had pneumonia, then the flu, no doubt brought on by an immune system ravaged by too much job stress and too little sleep, just like everyone else.*

"Do you remember when you used to wear high heels?" *Yes, I remember. If I decide that I want to go clomping in them down memory lane with you, I'll let you know.*

"Did you know that you're getting a mustache?" *Yes, I'm aware of that. I look at myself in the mirror every day.*

These were the questions that were asked and the answers that I never gave, but wanted to. I also wanted to tell people that unless they were preparing to sleep with me or had the letters M.D. after their name, they had no business touching my hair, my face, or my body unless I asked them to.

There's something about transition that gives folks the impression that they have free rein with your person and with your psyche. I've heard pregnant women complain that strangers walk up to them and touch their protruding abdomens as if they were small animals in a petting zoo. My friends walked up to me and ran their fingers through my hair to comment on my haircut, pointed at or touched my face to comment on my facial hair, and grabbed my arm to feel my muscle. They did these things without asking, as if I was such an anomaly that manners weren't even necessary anymore.

One male acquaintance was constantly slapping me on the back, for no reason that I could discern other than in some misguided attempt to show me that he believed I was "one of the boys." Another thought nothing of walking up within inches of my face and examining it for facial hair.

Even though I had been male in all areas of my life for several years, friends seemed to take it upon themselves to constantly remind me of the "good old days," or to comment that my "sex change" might have something to do with my stress, any illness that I contracted, or the fact that my car kept breaking down. I felt like a monkey in a zoo, existing only for their amusement or fascination, and they sometimes seemed to think exactly the same thing. And although I never said to them, "Remember when you were fat?" or "Oh, you seem to be losing your hair," although I didn't intimately examine their bodies, poke at them as if they were dead squirrels lying on the sidewalk, or invade their personal space to inspect them more closely, they seemed to have no problem with the reverse.

I was suddenly public property, and the whole idea was made even more disconcerting by the fact that they were all being so incredibly supportive. They were taking an interest in me, they were paying attention, and they cared, making it doubly difficult to be offended or to come up with a decently searing retort to an intrusive question.

Transpeople are a curiosity to others, and there's no way out of it. Even those who didn't know me before my transition think nothing of asking me intimate questions when they find out that I'm trans, as if I'm not quite human after all. Those who did know me before, and know that I was human once, now apparently have their doubts, since they seem perfectly comfortable asking those same intimate questions. Because I've chosen to be public about who I am, I don't mind sharing pieces of myself with others, to educate them and, hopefully, to dispel some myths and prejudices. But being asked about my genitalia during a question-and-answer session in a human sexuality class is different from being asked about it over lunch in a local restaurant.

The problem is that it's difficult to encourage and discourage questioning at the same time. I believe that transpeople will never be accepted and will never garner the same rights as nontranspeople if we don't talk about ourselves, tell our stories, and educate the world. When we're "out," we sacrifice some of our privacy, and that's a choice we have to make. Sometimes I feel as if I've sacrificed too much. Other times, I'm angry that nontranspeople don't know as much as they should, and I realize that the only way they'll ever know is for me to tell them. So I do. And I'll continue to walk that thin line between education and public display for as long as it takes other people to get it.

Maybe I'll damage myself in the process. Maybe I'll reveal things I can never take back. But maybe because of that, someone else—a little transperson not even born yet—will eventually benefit. And that will be what I can leave for the world.

A HYPOCRITICAL OATH

Not everyone who identifies as transgendered or gender diverse feels the need to transition. For those who do, it's a major step that can sometimes disrupt lives and lead to the breakup of relationships, the loss of a job, and personal safety risks. And it's expensive. In the United States, the vast majority of health insurance policies openly spell out their refusal to cover hormones and surgery. The cost of hormones can run into several hundred dollars a year, and the various surgeries can range from several thousand dollars to tens of thousands of dollars. A female-to-male transsexual who undergoes chest reconstruction, a complete hysterectomy, and a complete phalloplasty in the United States can end up spending as much as $100,000—sometimes more.

Many countries with universal health care systems will offer the surgeries at little or no cost, but they often will perform only a specified number per year, and the waiting list is long. There are many transpeople who want to transition, but simply can't afford it. And because a therapist's letter is required for both hormones and surgery, those without health insurance in the United States often can't even afford the therapy needed to get the letter.

But hormones and surgery are only half the story. Transsexual people need routine medical care. We get pneumonia, we break bones, we cut ourselves, we get cancer, we have heart attacks—just like everyone else. We are not so alien that "normal" human maladies don't befall us. And when they do, we need the same types of treatment that everyone else receives. Sometimes we get them. Sometimes we don't.

The current health care system in the United States is set up to let most people down, but transsexual people are especially vulnerable. We bear some of the responsibility. Many female-to-males simply can't stand the thought of going to the gynecologist, although it's absolutely necessary for those who still have female organs. While very few nontranswomen are comfortable with this intimate invasion of privacy, it can feel like a special violation to a transman. Even with the most understanding gynecologist, the intrusive pelvic exam and Pap test serve as reminders of what we have and what we don't have—and of our female history.

For those who identify as men, this exercise in humiliation is often so unbearable that they forego yearly exams altogether—a certain invitation to trouble. And those in smaller towns, where very little is confidential, or those who are at the mercy of uninformed, uneducated, or even prejudiced doctors and nurses, are unlikely to follow through with regular medical care. But we have to do it. We have to be responsible for taking the initiative with our own health care—because no one else will.

Yes, it's embarrassing to make an appointment with an ob/gyn in a baritone voice. Yes, it's embarrassing to sit in the waiting room in a full beard. I pretend I'm waiting for my wife until I'm called in. Once, the nurse called me up to the desk and asked, rather loudly, in a waiting room full of women, why I was there. In the most casual voice I could muster, I said, "Pap test and pelvic exam." She said, "Oh," and I sat back down, almost smugly. Leave 'em wondering, I always say.

I do my best to maintain regular and adequate health care—in spite of the system. But taking care of our bodies and maintaining our health are often more difficult goals than they should be. There is a great deal of prejudice in the medical establishment with regard to transpeople. Routine and even emergency medical care is sometimes impossible to get, and the attitudes of medical professionals toward trans patients have cost some their lives.

In 1995, Tyra Hunter, a male-to-female transsexual, died after a car accident when emergency medical technicians discovered her penis and discontinued treatment at the scene, choosing instead to laugh and make jokes while onlookers pleaded with them to help her. And in 1999, Robert Eads, a female-to-male transsexual, died of ovarian cancer after over twenty doctors refused to see him, saying that they didn't want to deal with him or that they didn't want him sitting in their waiting room. Information about these cases and others can be found at the Remembering Our Dead Web site (www.gender.org/remember). Robert Eads's final year was recorded by filmmaker Kate Davis in the award-winning film *Southern Comfort*. These are documented cases of medical neglect resulting in death.

I was told by an angry doctor in my HMO that I was going to die if I didn't stop taking my hormones, even though there was nothing in the minor problems I was experiencing to indicate this outcome. I didn't stop taking them and, to paraphrase Mark Twain, reports of my impending death were obviously greatly exaggerated. But I could tell from my doctor's apparent rage that she didn't find me appealing and that she was having a difficult time working with me. Although I've never been denied care, there are many others who have, as evidenced by the examples above, and this is only the short list.

Medical professionals should know better. They've taken an oath to provide the best possible treatment for all. There should not be categories of people who aren't eligible for appropriate medical care. One of the biggest fears that transsexual people have is of getting sick and having to be hospitalized. To be at the mercy of an uncaring, and sometimes hateful, health care system is terrifying. The deaths of Tyra Hunter and Robert Eads were preventable. There is no excuse for what happened to them, and there is no excuse for the continued neglect of transpeople at the hands of medical professionals who are entrusted to save lives, not take them.

To be fair, there are many medical professionals who are completely open and at ease with treating transpeople. Some even specifically market to the trans community, knowing that their services are needed and welcomed. There are many more who at least tolerate us and would never consider denying us care. Unfortunately, there are still not enough, and those transpeople who do not have the resources to seek out compassionate health care providers or who are left helpless in emergency situations where they must take what they can get are sometimes paying the ultimate price.

As transpeople, we take our bodies to a level that we're comfortable with in our transition, then we take care of them as best we can and go off and live our lives. Those lives are usually pretty insignificant if you use the universe and infinity as standards of measurement, but they are ours nonetheless and we have a right to them. In the last half decade of my life, I seem to have offended a great many people just by existing. I've been told that I have no right to do what I did and that I have no right to change my body as I have. It's amazing how indignant people can become when someone who they have never seen before and will never see again does something that has no effect on their lives whatsoever. The people closest to me have been able to accept my changed body. They've been able to deal with my experience and what they have experienced in the process. Their feelings, and what I think about myself, are really what's most important.

But I still need medical help, just like everyone else. I still need to feel safe, just like everyone else. And I should be able to look to my future without worry about whether or not I will receive the proper care in sickness and old age—or at least without any more worry than anyone else has about these things. I pay my taxes, I pay my insurance premiums and deductibles, I vote, and I obey the law. I'm a citizen of the United States, and I'm entitled to the same rights as everyone else in my country. I have the same responsibilities, too. That's just being human. I hope that someday my society will see it that way.

PART FOUR

trans sexuality

sexual transsexuals

Transsexuality is the business of being transsexual. Trans sexuality is the business of being sexual. Being transsexual doesn't have a whole lot to do with the act of sex, although I'm sure that there are some transpeople out there who are getting a whole lot luckier than I am. The "sex" part of "transsexual" refers to biological sex or social gender—the maleness or femaleness of someone. "Trans" means to go across or to change. Therefore, transsexual means to go across or change sexes or genders and has no relationship to physical intimacy or attraction.

I am frequently asked, "Who do transsexual people have sex with?" Presumably, this is a legitimate question, since we're assumed to be an alternate species and therefore incapable of completing the sex act with anyone who is not from Alpha Centauri. The answer, of course, is that transsexual people have sex with their partners, their one-night-stands, or whoever they have chosen to have sex with. Transsexual people have sex organs, regardless of what surgeries they have or haven't had. We still have orgasms (another question I've been asked). We are as creative with our sexuality and our sexual activities as anyone else. And in most cases, our gender identification has very little to do with our sexual orientation.

Gender identity is the term used to describe how a person feels about him- or herself—what gender that person feels he or she is.

Sexual orientation is the term used to describe that person's attractions—what sex/gender/hair color/eye color/body build/personality that person is physically and emotionally drawn to. Once that distinction is made, another confusion follows rapidly on its heels —"If sexual orientation doesn't change, how could you be straight as a woman and gay as a man? You changed your sexual orientation." In fact, I did not—my label just changed.

People are sexually oriented to men, to women, to both, to certain people, regardless of their sex or gender, or to no one. Yes, this does leave out those who will date only someone from Alpha Centauri, but they are few and far between and, for anyone who's interested, they can usually be found at *Star Trek* conventions. "Gay," "lesbian," "straight," and "bisexual" are labels, not orientations. And the interesting thing is that these labels are applied based not on the gender a person is attracted to, but on the gender of the person feeling the attraction. As a female, I was considered "straight." As a male, I'm considered "gay." My sexual orientation, which is to men, hasn't changed. My label has changed because my own gender has changed. My label has nothing to do with who I'm attracted to. It has everything to do with who I am.

When I announced my decision to transition to male after living over four decades of my life as a straight female, my friends reacted with shock and dismay. Their first concern was what I would do with my wardrobe, complete with several pairs of four-inch spiked heels. Their second was who would get what (and that was just the guys). After they finished fighting over my Donna Karan blazers, they actually began thinking about the finer points of gender reassignment—like who I would sleep with.

"So you like women now?" one of my female friends asked, eyeing me as if the testosterone would kick in at any moment and I would be compelled to lunge at her.

"No," I said. "Why should I?"

She seemed relieved but still suspicious. "Well, you're straight, aren't you?"

She wasn't the only one who mistook a label for a sexual orientation. Several others asked me if I was going to start dating women, since, of course, everyone knew I was straight. Therein lies the question that our species has been grappling with since the dawn of time—if a straight female undergoes gender reassignment, what, then, is his sexual orientation when he comes out on the other side?

I can't speak for the multitudes, but I can tell you that my primary sexual orientation is, and always has been, to men. Whether that makes me gay, straight, or something else entirely is a question best left to those whose job it is to come up with labels. But with the limited sexualities that our culture defines, as a female attracted to men, I was straight. As a male lusting after the same guys, I'm gay.

This amazing concept helps explain my ability to easily change sexual orientations, a feat that has yet to be accomplished by anyone in Exodus International. I didn't change orientations, only labels. However, I soon discovered that calling myself a gay man didn't go over well with one particular population—gay men.

Some gay men have become mightily offended when I've called myself a gay man. Ironically, the men who get the angriest with me when I mention that the "gay community" tends to be phallically oriented are the first to insist that I can't call myself a man because I don't have a penis. They go on to tell me that I'm not gay because I haven't had the "gay experience" in my life.

I'll grant them that I don't have a penis (unless I count the collection in my underwear drawer). I'll also concede that I didn't have the "gay experience" when I was growing up, even though that experience is probably quite different for someone growing up in the heart of San Francisco and someone growing up in the heart of rural Nebraska. The only problem I have is with the cumbersome language that it takes to actually describe myself—a transsexual man who is primarily attracted to men. "Gay man" is so much easier to say.

In truth, I prefer to describe myself as "sexual." Almost everyone is sexual in some way, and it allows for quite a bit of leeway. It also doesn't come with a host of expectations about what I'm going to be like in my everyday life—with my clothes *on*. But in this culture, it's expected that I'll put a "hetero," "homo," or "bi" in front of the word, and calling myself "sexual" sometimes leads others to believe that my sex life falls somewhere between that of Casanova and the Marquis de Sade. Since this is hardly the case, I generally revert back to the label "gay transman," which doesn't offend those who know that I'm phallically challenged, and which at least gives me a little mystery and excitement in the company of those who don't understand the term at all.

Suddenly being gay, or at least being considered as such, has been an interesting adjustment. So has loosening my grip on the straight mainstream's idea of sexuality. I've often considered how much easier it would be if sexual orientation could be changed, if the label constituted the loving and I could be as "straight" in my new body as I was in my old one. Holding hands with a woman while walking down the street, putting my arm around her at the movies, giving her a kiss at the mall—all would put me right back into the comfortable, acceptable world from which I came. And it might be easier for me to find a partner.

Many straight- and lesbian-identified women have no problem dating a transman. There are even some women who seek out transmen as partners. They're attracted to the male physical attributes and are equally drawn to the fact that transmen have experienced aspects of femaledom that a nontransmale will never know. This boyfriend knows how to treat a woman, has a healthy respect for her, and knows what she wants, sexually and otherwise, because he's been there. Whether or not he has a penis doesn't seem to be a major issue. But as logical as this arrangement might appear, especially for a transman like me, my sexual orientation has remained unchanged and I've kept my gay transman label.

It's not that I didn't have the opportunity to change. Although sex was on my mind immediately after my first shot of testosterone, I at once discovered the paradox of female-to-male transition—at the beginning of transition, when the newly introduced male hormones create insatiable physical desire, you yourself are at your least desirable. I was at the point in my transition where straight men no longer looked at me, and although gay men sometimes glanced with interest, they turned away when they decided that I was either a thirteen-year-old boy or a very masculine woman. I was, however, attracting a totally new crop of admirers that I knew absolutely nothing about—lesbian women.

The woman from the gas company actually held some promise in her rough-and-tumble masculinity. She was round and jovial and not the least bit concerned that she'd been called to my house in the middle of the night because my pilot light was out.

"I'm really sorry," I said, wringing my hands and stuttering, because I truly was sorry. What man wouldn't know how to light his oven? But she saw through that macho manly act right away.

"It's okay," she said, giving me a smile that was half mother, half seductress. "This is my job. Look, I'll show you. Come down here. Look."

She was already on her knees, and I carefully lowered myself beside her. When we were both on the floor and peering into the oven, our heads nearly touching, she expertly lit the pilot light, then beamed. *Woman with fire*, I thought. *Not a bad catch.*

But there was another problem as well—a metal panel in the bottom of the oven was bent. Whether or not it had any effect on the pilot light was never quite established. But it was obviously important enough that she nudged me out of the way with her broad shoulders and lifted the offending panel out of the oven. Then she stomped on the wobbly metal with her boot until it was bent back into place, all the while smiling as if she were slaying a dragon just for me. *Woman with strength. Could come in very handy.*

After she had repaired everything there was to repair and commented on my beautiful apartment, she stood for a moment, still smiling, still looking at me, and I wondered if I was supposed to do something. Then she said, "Now if that happens again, you just feel free to call. Any time. I work nights so late night isn't an issue."

The fact that she had taught me how to light the pilot myself didn't seem to matter. I was to call if it happened again. I later figured out that this might have meant that I was to call if I wanted to see her again, but I was too dumb to get it. No woman had ever flirted with me before. The next time the pilot light went out, I lit it myself, which was actually to her benefit. By that time, my breasts were gone and my facial hair had started to struggle up through the mutated follicles. I think she would have been disappointed.

She wasn't the only lesbian who showed some interest in the beginning of my transition. And although I had no idea how to flirt with women, and even less of an idea of how to have sex with one, there are times now that I wish I had tried it out when I had the chance. I might be "gay," but I'm all for keeping my options open.

Not everyone maintains the same types of attractions once they transition. Some people actually do get over to "the other side" and discover that their attractions have changed. There are any number of explanations for this, and each person's experience is different. One possible reason for a transman to be attracted to men as a female and to women as a male is that he does, in fact, have a "straight" identity or way of seeing the world, and heterosexual sex is the most natural and attractive to him. Another is that he might have had female attractions all along, but was unable to recognize or act on them because of our society's strong homophobia, which he probably internalized as well. Or he might only feel comfortable interacting with women as a man. It's also possible for someone with a homosexual orientation before transition to continue a homosexual orientation after transition. Some people feel that it's more comfortable or natural for them to be with a person of their own sex or gender. Hormones can also be tricky little devils. People respond to them differently, and they can cause mental, as well as physical, changes.

No matter what the reasons, it's still important to understand that sexual orientation is not a choice. Attractions come naturally and we have little control over them. Anyone who has ever fallen in love—with anyone—knows that he or she had very little choice in the matter. And I am living, breathing proof of that fact. There was a time in my life when I would have given my right breast to be a lesbian. It would have explained a lot of anguish that I was going through with my gender identity issues. In fact, my attraction to men was what kept me in the dark for so long. "You can't be a man," I would tell myself whenever the gender problems surfaced. "You're attracted to men." It took over forty years to realize that sexual orientation and gender identity aren't the same thing, and in many cases have nothing to do with each other at all.

My existence and my proclivities are also handy for dismissing another widely held notion—that transsexuals undergo gender reassignment to deny their homosexuality. That makes about as much sense as the idea that a lung cancer patient has a lung removed to deny the fact that he needs to breathe. In reality, he would undergo this painful and frightening operation in order to keep breathing, to keep living, just as transsexuals want to keep living in bodies that will allow them to do so. Expensive, complicated surgeries and sometimes dangerous hormone administration are not undertaken by someone just to make his or her sexual attractions more acceptable. Anyone who would submit to such a project has an unshakeable identification with a gender other than the one assigned at birth.

It didn't take me long to understand all this once I began to live it, but unfortunately, society as a whole is way behind. I don't have a problem with my sexual orientation, whatever label is put on it. I know what it is and I live it every day. My life as a gay transman is full and satisfying. The fact that I'm sometimes more acceptable to the mainstream straight community than I am to the gay and lesbian community is my only confusion. Especially since it seems to me that we're all in this together.

YOU SAY GLB, I SAY GLBT

In recent years, some transsexual people, regardless of sexual orientation, have aligned with the gay and lesbian community and have requested (or demanded) inclusion in that "movement." Many gay and lesbian organizations have agreed, and have changed their names and mission statements to include transgendered and transsexual people—they have added "T" to "GLB." The most progressive organizations have had it there all along. But others have not been so receptive. In fact, the "T" does belong there. For all of us—gay, lesbian, bisexual, and trans—it's about gender. It's not about the gender we're attracted to—it's about the gender we are.

Unfortunately, it's been a hard sell. Many in the gay and lesbian community have rejected transfolk in the larger scheme of things, arguing that our two communities have nothing in common and that "weird" and "crazy" transpeople will destroy the credibility of the mainstream GLB movement. They're wrong. The two communities have much in common, because we share a common problem—we are all discriminated against because of our gender.

First, we're discriminated against because of our gender presentation. Transpeople who are born with male bodies but are really female are discriminated against because they present a female gender. Transpeople who are born with female bodies but are really male are discriminated against because they present a male gender.

Gay men and lesbians also experience the same kind of discrimination. Research has shown that the majority of people who exhibit "gender-variant" behaviors in childhood (i.e., "feminine" boys and "masculine" girls) grow up to identify as gay or lesbian, not as trans. As these children get older, they are singled out, harassed, and physically assaulted based on their appearance and behaviors—their gender presentation—and not on their sexual orientation. Unless someone comes out as gay or lesbian, his or her sexual orientation is unknown. The harassment and the discrimination are based on *perceived* sexual orientation—perceived through that person's gender presentation. The same thing happens to straight children and straight adults who do not present an "acceptable" masculine or feminine gender.

If a man is walking down the street alone—no rainbow flags, no T-shirt with a cute saying, just walking—and a stranger leans out of the car window and yells "Fag," it's not because this stranger knows the man's sexual orientation. It's because of the way the man is presenting his gender. It's in the way he's walking or the clothes he's wearing. He's presenting his gender in a way that's inconsistent with what's expected of a straight American male—and because of this, he's perceived as gay. He might be gay. He might not be. But he's *perceived* as gay because of his gender presentation.

If a gay man or a lesbian interviews for a job and doesn't get that job, he or she might believe it has something to do with sexual orientation. And it might. But if sexual orientation isn't discussed in the interview—and it shouldn't be—the only reason that it could be a factor is because of gender presentation. If this person is presenting his or her gender in a nontraditional way, the assumption is that he is gay or she is a lesbian. The discrimination isn't due to sexual orientation. It's due to *perceived* sexual orientation based on gender expression. Transpeople? Well, none of those applicants even got to the first interview. But the point is that we're all judged on our gender presentation.

Even the comment "Gosh, you don't seem gay" is based on the way a person is expressing his or her gender and the expectations that go with gender expression and sexual orientation. Our society has come to expect that gay men and lesbians will express their gender differently from straight people, and when they don't, it's always a surprise to some members of the straight community. "How could you be gay? You're so masculine. How could you be a lesbian? You're so feminine." Even that is discrimination.

And many gay and lesbian people see and understand this type of discrimination—even those who insist that our communities have nothing in common. In a sampling of gay and lesbian personal ads, there's bound to be the words "straight acting" in one or more of the offerings. But how does a straight person act? How does a gay person act? This acknowledgement, by gay men and lesbians, that there is some way to "act straight" is, in itself, a reflection of the gender bias that unites us all under a common flag. The inference that it is somehow *better* to act straight is also an acknowledgment of the gender bias that we face. The discrimination is there, based on gender and gender expression, and those who feel the necessity to differentiate between how gay people act and how straight people act are the ones who should see it the most. Unfortunately, they're often the ones who are the most transphobic. They have so carefully constructed their gender presentation as a defense against societal prejudice that they're afraid that associating with transpeople will destroy the façade.

Another reason that the T belongs with GLB is that we are all discriminated against because of our bodies—our bodies don't match the traditional expectations of gender in our society, which are that "man" equals "penis" and "woman" equals "vagina." Trans bodies certainly don't match these expectations. A woman with a penis? A man with a vagina? Sorry, no (fill in the blank here—job, apartment, loan, insurance, benefits, wedding) for you.

But gay and lesbian bodies are "correct," right? They're "normal," right? But they still don't match the gender expectations of our society. Two penises in bed? Sorry. Two vaginas in the shower? Uh uh. Gay men and lesbians are being discriminated against because they turned up with the wrong body parts—the parts that match those of the person they fell in love with. Remember, it's not the gender you love that's the problem. It's the gender *you are*.

The other argument, that transpeople are "weird" and "crazy," is the same argument that has been used for years against GLB people, especially by the religious Right. In 1972, gay men and lesbians were as nuts as I am. They're okay now only because the American Psychiatric Association (APA) voted to remove homosexuality from the *DSM* in 1973. If a person with a penis wearing a dress is weird and crazy, I wonder about all the drag shows I see when I go to gay bars—and I won't even talk about Halloween. And what's up with the drag king shows that are attended primarily by lesbians? It seems that transgendered presentations are acceptable to a point, as long as they wash off at the end of the night.

Of course, not all GLB people exhibit gender-variant behaviors or appearance. Nor do all transpeople. I know some extremely masculine men and some very feminine women who have corrected the physical mistake of their birth and who identify as straight, mainstream men and women. They would no sooner desire to be included in the GLB movement than would Newt Gingrich. That would be far too "weird" and "crazy" for them. But even *they* don't have the right to marry who they choose, can get fired from their job or dismissed from the military, and risk getting beat up or even killed because of who they are. We have the same issues.

Gay men, lesbians, bisexual people, transfolk—we all have something in common. The core of our commonality is gender—we are labeled and discriminated against based on our gender. The second layer is the form that discrimination takes—murders, assaults, destruction of property, failure to get jobs or housing, inadequate health care, the inability to marry, the denial of partner benefits, and society's narrow definition of "family" that doesn't include us. And while I'm busy trying to convince some gay men and lesbians of this concept, I am equally engaged in trying to convince some transfolk of the same thing.

Yes, transphobia runs rampant in the gay and lesbian community, but there is no lack of homophobia in the trans community either. While some gay men and lesbians are scared off by any association with transfolk, some, maybe even the majority, of transpeople feel the same way. They identify as straight, have assimilated into the larger mainstream community, and want no association with the "fringe" element that they consider the gay and lesbian population to be. They buy into both arguments that the GLB community has established—that we have nothing in common and, that by aligning with the GLB community, our own quest for equal rights will not succeed.

Take a look:

"I don't want to look like a faggot."

"Is there no getting away from you people?"

"I'm not going to a gay bar. I'm not a fag."

These are actual comments to which I have been subjected—by transmen. Homophobia isn't relegated to the straight nontrans population. It's alive and well in my own trans community, a community that ought to know better. I've had some transmen gape in disbelief when they find out I'm gay. I've heard others say that they want nothing to do with the gay and lesbian community. "Those people are just too weird," they say.

Oh, please. Like being a transman is as mainstream as shopping malls and cell phones. Coming out as gay in the trans community can be as difficult as coming out as trans in the nontrans community. There are transmen who feel that any alliance with the gay and lesbian community is wrong and can only lead to trouble. They've transitioned into straight, middle-class lives with wives and children. They want no identification with a population that they see as "different" or "deviant." Never mind that they suffer the same discriminations as gay men and lesbians. Never mind that, in most states, the straight marriages they cherish are really considered same-sex marriages and could be invalidated in a heartbeat if their birth sex was discovered. Never mind that, when they die, their wills can be contested and their wives left with nothing. Never mind that there are transmen who have been left to die—just like many gay men with AIDS or many lesbians with ovarian or breast cancer—because they couldn't get appropriate medical treatment, especially for nonmale illnesses. Never mind that they could be denied housing, loans, or jobs if their birth sex came to light.

Medical treatment, property rights, marriage, jobs, housing—these are the issues of gay and lesbian politics. These are issues that assimilated transmen feel are their birthright—but they sometimes forget what their original birth certificate said.

Homophobia in the trans community is not just an inconvenience for transpeople who are subjected to homophobic remarks. It's dangerous and deadly. It prevents us from joining with the one community that, when it's not wallowing in its own transphobia, might help make a difference with legislation that will benefit us. It prevents us from joining in our own community as a solidified political block. It's imperative that we join together and remain united—GLBT and anyone else who wants to come on board—so that we can use our numbers to tear down the discrimination that all of us face because of our gender.

But with so much animosity going on between various factions in various communities, wouldn't it just be easier if transpeople kept to themselves and joined with their "own kind"? It might be, but in many cases, the only thing transpeople have in common is the fact that they are trans. Transfolk come from so many backgrounds and have so many varied interests, hobbies, and political, religious, and social affiliations that, like anyone else, they tend to gravitate toward groups and individuals who share their beliefs, opinions, and lifestyle choices. A fifty-year-old Republican transwoman would probably have little in common with a twenty-year-old Democratic transman, and people can only discuss their surgeries for so long before they start to nod off.

I've often been asked if I would consider having a relationship with another transman, as if our similar genitalia would make us the perfect pair. Early in my transition, I refused to even entertain the idea. I wanted a man with a penis—not just any old penis, but a fully functioning, natural one. In my previous life, I had loved every aspect of maledom (with the exception of beer guts, hairy backs, and the idea that farting is hilarious), and I was especially fascinated by the nifty parlor tricks displayed by this particular male organ. This jack-of-all-trades allowed for standing elimination, sexual interaction, and was, in the case of some of my former lovers, the perfect bite-sized after-dinner treat. It could go from alpha sleep to a twenty-one-gun salute in a matter of seconds. It provided hours of entertainment—far better than solitaire, although it could, and often did, play that game in my absence. It even re-created itself in gizmos such as remote controls and bright red sports cars, no doubt designed by natal men. And it was never sexier than when it was perky and ready for action, outlined in a tight pair of jeans.

Not only was a factory-equipped penis a nonnegotiable requirement for a partner, but I also knew that any future lover would have to have lived his entire life as a male. I have nothing against females. Some of my best friends used to be females. Some still are. It was simply the idea of maleness—male energy, male bodies, and male psyches—that triggered responses in the reptilian part of my brain. I knew who I was and I knew what I wanted. Being less than perfect myself didn't seem to affect my choosiness in any way.

At the time, I had met only a few transmen, most of whom were just beginning their own transitions and so showed little of the masculine traits that I found attractive. I simply couldn't picture myself with someone so much like me. Part of this, certainly, was my insecurity about my own masculinity, but I held firm (or maybe not so firm) in my belief that a biological penis attached to a masculine, male-born man was the only way to go—until I attended my first major female-to-male conference.

When we drove up to the hotel in Los Angeles, I was pretty sure that we were in the right place. Two of my friends and I had driven cross-country for twenty-four hours straight to get to the FtM conference put on through FTM International, the largest female-to-male organization in the world. In true female fashion, I had developed a bladder infection along the way and was chugging cranberry juice from the bottle when we pulled up to see an assortment of short guys standing outside the hotel. Yup, we were in the right place. I had recently had my chest surgery and it made everything about the trip that much more exciting. I could wear T-shirts without a bulky layer on top to disguise my breasts. And just before going to the hotel, we had actually gone to the beach and I had taken my shirt off—right there, on an LA beach. And I had frolicked. What else could I do, once I had my shirt off? Frolicking seemed like the only legitimate choice.

The lobby was buzzing, crowded with conference-goers standing in line to register or talking in small groups. And as I looked around me, pretty much all I saw were men—men with beards, men with mustaches, men with muscles, men with tattoos, men with low, mellow voices, and men with boisterous laughs. Who were all these men? Where had they come from? In theory, I knew that they were out there. I had networked with them on the Internet. But to see them all in one place—over four hundred of them—and to stand in the middle of their masculinity was almost overwhelming. It was so much more powerful than seeing them in the pages of a book or reading their stories on some computer screen.

In reality, not all of these men probably identified as such, but based on their outward appearance, no one who walked into that lobby would have seen anything other than a large group of men. No one who wasn't there for the conference would have ever suspected that these men had been born female.

Some were balding, from years of testosterone use and a male pattern baldness gene that I was hoping I didn't have. Some had thick beards and potbellies, a collection of Santa Clauses at various ages. Some were thin and sinewy, others were swollen with muscle. I saw conservative men dressed in neatly pressed khakis and button-down shirts or polos. I saw men with shaved and tattooed heads, with nose rings and eyebrow rings and rows of silver studs along each ear. There were men with breasts who looked like women and there were men with breasts who looked like men. The breasts would have been the only giveaway. And there were men who were absolutely gorgeous.

The conference program was filled with workshops. During some hours, there were as many as ten selections to choose from, ranging from activism to sexuality to hormones and surgery, and from FtM history to spirituality. There were 12-Step meetings, workshops for partners, workshops for older men, and workshops for teens. There were sessions for FtM parents and parents of FtMs. We could learn about sex toys or male mannerisms or how to pee standing up. Specialized workshops dealt with issues for Jewish FtMs or FtMs of Color or those who were differently abled. In a pumping workshop, I witnessed the presenter apply a penis pump to his former clitoris and pump it up to a good two to three inches. Surgeons, therapists, and endocrinologists traveled cross-country to present workshops and to garner business. And in addition to the workshops, we could peruse the vendor area, where books, T-shirts, and pants stuffers were for sale. In the evening, there were parties, which included an onstage version of *The Dating Game*, comedy, and musical entertainment. And every time I looked around me, there were men. And it's likely that the majority of them didn't have penises.

And because I had been so insistent on my specific requirements for all potential partners, of course I got the hots for a sexy transman.

I had no idea that transmen were such hot stuff until that magic moment, across the proverbial crowded room, when I swear that even my soft silicone pants stuffer was standing at attention. At that instant, I knew that I wanted to sleep with the guy and I couldn't care less what he had in his pants or what sex was written on his original birth certificate.

Nothing happened with this guy and nothing ever will, but that doesn't matter. What was important about the discovery was that it not only changed the way I viewed other transmen, it changed the way I viewed myself. It opened up a whole other world of potential partners. It opened my mind to the idea of "queer sex," not necessarily defined by the boundaries of man-woman, woman-woman, or man-man. It made me realize that a relationship between two people, sexual or otherwise, has little to do with genitalia or bodies. I finally understood that the brain truly is the biggest and most erotic sexual organ. And I also understood that people, regardless of their sex or gender, who insist on a penis being naturally attached to their partners are definitely missing a whole dimension of sexual and romantic experience.

I will always be attracted to maleness. However, my definition of maleness and what I find attractive were forever altered by this experience. For that, my fellow traveler in this gender journey, who shall remain anonymous, I thank you.

To date (or not to date), I have not been with a transperson romantically or sexually. I have a lot of trans friends and I'm very active in the transgender "movement," which is happening in our country and in the world, no matter who we join with politically or otherwise. And, although I still call myself "gay," it's primarily for the benefit of people who feel the need for a one-word definition of my sexuality.

At this point, I haven't eliminated anyone from my potential partner list based on gender identification or expression, and genitalia is simply a nonissue. There are so many other wonderful, interesting things about people. There are so many reasons to get to know someone besides what we *think* might be in his or her pants (after reading this, you'll never be completely certain again). If we could all just forget about genitalia and move on to the really important stuff in life, perhaps we could all live together a little more harmoniously. And for those who are so focused on penises and vaginas, on who has what, and who they should love, and what rights they should or shouldn't have because of it—get your mind out of the gutter.

WHaT Does THaT MaKe Me?

No matter how we're viewed by society, no matter where we fit in (or don't), most transpeople are involved in various personal relationships, and these relationships have many opportunities to go askew before, during, and after transition. One of the things that transpeople often fail to realize and fail to deal with is that a transition, for many of those on the outside looking in, is almost like a death. A loved one is dying and friends and family members are helpless to do anything but stand by and watch. Those closest to us sometimes actually go through the five stages that Dr. Elisabeth Kübler-Ross made so famous.

Denial: "You're changing your gender? That's ridiculous. You're so feminine/masculine. Of course you're not going to do that. Are you sure you're not just gay?"

Anger: "Why didn't you tell me this before? How long have you known about this? You haven't been honest with me. Why are you doing this *to me*?"

Bargaining: "Maybe there's some way to fix this. We just need to get you the right help. I'll be a better wife/husband/partner/parent/child. You don't want to hurt the children, do you?"

Depression: "I can't deal with it. You need to leave. I'm sorry, but can't you see that I'm hurting, too? You're not my son/daughter/mother/father/spouse/partner anymore."

Acceptance: Sometimes it happens. Sometimes it doesn't.

Of course, not all loved ones go through this. It's surprising the number of people who aren't surprised. In many cases, parents have already seen the signs. Some spouses or partners have as well. And even those who haven't noticed the signals often come to acceptance very quickly. Each situation and each person is different. And there are never any guarantees. Many transpeople have caring and supportive loved ones. Many others have been rejected or even disowned by family and friends. As an alternative, transpeople have often banded together to celebrate holidays and other important events, and have developed new "families" to share their lives. But time has a way of working in our favor, and relatives and friends often come around and begin to accept us back into their lives—sometimes after many years. We just do the best we can and we try to maintain as many of our existing relationships as possible while cultivating new ones along the way.

The whole ordeal can be especially difficult for spouses and partners. Many transpeople are involved in a romantic and sexual relationship before transition. Some relationships do not survive it. Some grow stronger. But even those who are fully supportive and intend to stick by their transitioning partner through and after transition have a lot of questions.

One of the most important, and most confusing, questions that partners seem to have is "What does that make me?" Because we're so attached to our labels of sexual orientation, a partner wants to know how the transition will affect his or her label as a heterosexual or a homosexual person. Transmen are often in relationships with women before transition, and those women usually see that relationship as a lesbian one. Some transmen, however, see the same relationship as heterosexual. Even as females, they felt male, and therefore saw themselves as a male in a partnership with a female.

For those transmen, the whole thing is a natural progression. The lesbian partner, however, sometimes feels that she is losing her identity. She is used to a community—the lesbian community. She is used to being treated and viewed a certain way. Now, suddenly, she will be seen by the world as a straight female. In a few cases, both the lesbian woman and her transman partner are rejected by the very community they have settled in and are comfortable in, because now they are a "straight" couple. This readjustment to the world and how they are seen by others can sometimes seriously damage a relationship. But many women are able to maintain their lesbian identity in this type of relationship and are able to separate society's view of them as a "straight" female from their own knowledge of who they really are.

Nontransmen have a much more difficult time accepting the transition of their female partner to male, and the majority of these relationships do not survive. Much of society still takes a dim view of gay men, and these once-heterosexual men would now be seen as gay, something that's very difficult for some of them to deal with. Also, because men tend to be more visually attracted to their partners, the change is often too drastic for them. The physical arousal, and even the feelings of tenderness and romance, that happened with a female partner are simply not there anymore.

Although women are also visually attracted to their partners, often the emotional connection takes precedence. There are far more women who stay with their transitioning male-to-female partners than the other way around. But even these women sometimes go through the confusion of wondering whether or not they are now lesbians—in society's eyes, they might very well be. But what really matters is how they see themselves and if they are able to live comfortably with that identity.

Another concern partners have involves personality and behavioral changes brought about by hormones. They don't know what to expect, and it's frightening to think that their familiar partner might become a stranger. Does transitioning cause major personality changes? Maybe.

I believe that a person's core personality probably will not change. The horror stories that female partners of transmen have heard about hormones are usually just that—stories. Although some transmen profess to feel more aggressive during certain times when the hormone levels peak in their bodies, many say that they feel calmer and more in control after they're free from the monthly estrogen-induced mood swings. It's highly unlikely that hormones alone will turn a kind, mild-mannered, and monogamous individual into an abusive, rage-filled, and cheating partner. In fact, most people tend toward just the opposite. Comfort with one's body and with the way one is seen by and treated by the world can have extremely positive effects. Most transpeople, after transition, are happier, more fulfilled, and easier to get along with.

That said, there can be certain problems. Testosterone can substantially increase the sex drive, and although a faithful partner will usually remain just that, the increase in sexual desire can be exhausting to some female partners. They should wait it out—it levels off. Partners of transwomen might see different types of changes. Estrogen can affect mood and can make some transwomen more emotional. None of these things has to be negative, and they are usually minor glitches in the system until everyone adjusts.

But sometimes transpeople do seem to change because they are finally becoming who they have always wanted and needed to be—themselves. Transitioning is a growth process and growth involves change. Change can have a positive or a negative effect on any relationship, whether it involves a gender transition or not. As in any relationship, it's most important to keep the lines of communication open, be willing to listen, and be as open and honest as possible.

While transition can be a tedious time for everyone, there are some things that we as transpeople can do to make the process easier for those around us.

People in transition are often very self-absorbed without meaning to be. They are undergoing changes that they've waited a lifetime to experience and they sometimes forget that their excitement is not necessarily shared by those around them. Transitioning people are experiencing their own fears as well, which can make it difficult to recognize and respond to the fears of their loved ones.

For a period of time, friends and family might find that the transitioning person can think and talk of little other than the transition process and what's happening to him or her. This will pass, but it tends to be a miserable time for those who have to listen and can certainly alienate all but the transperson's staunchest supporters. I'm sure that there were many times when my friends were thinking, "If he tells me about that stupid shot one more time, there will definitely be some shooting and it won't be with a needle." We all survived, but it's something for transitioning people to keep in mind. They do have a great deal of control over how relationships with others are maintained during this period.

My advice to transpeople is to listen, listen, and listen some more. Your friends and family, and especially your spouse or partner, need to be heard, they need to have their feelings and fears recognized and acknowledged by you, and they need some downtime, some time away from the transition. Go to a movie, go on a picnic, do something that demonstrates that you are still the person they love and that you have more to talk about than the five hairs that are sprouting from your chin. Believe it or not, those hairs are not the stuff of engaging conversation.

The important thing for transpeople to remember when dealing with friends, family, partners, or complete strangers on the street is that most people will take their cues from us. If we see our transsexuality as shameful or disgusting, they will, too. If we see ourselves as sick or perverted, they will, too. If we're uncomfortable, we'll make those around us uncomfortable. But if we see ourselves as the normal, intelligent, diverse people that we are, and if we live our lives accordingly, with many interests and outlets other than just our transsexuality... well, I can't guarantee that everyone else will follow suit, but at least we'll have set the stage for acceptance by others and, most importantly, for our own self-acceptance. And if we take the time to *be* a loving partner in every way, we'll know that we've done everything we can to help the relationship succeed.

PART FIVE

Trans Pride

A MaTTer OF CHOICE

It might sound strange to take pride in something that has nothing to do with winning the Nobel Prize, saving a life, or discovering a cure for cancer, but cultivating self-pride is an important step for people who have been shunned, ridiculed, and basically treated just downright nastily for a long time. I've been called "sick" and I've been called "brave," but I don't believe I'm either. I'm just a person struggling to get by in the world, like everyone else, while dealing with life's little practical jokes. In my case, one of my issues, besides the fact that there is never enough money, that I'm getting older every day, and that mechanical things always break down, is that I'm a transsexual. It never goes away, just like impending death and yearly taxes. It's not a curse and I'm not a victim. It's just a fact.

We don't know why some people are trans. Maybe we'll never find out and, if we don't, does it matter? It's simply the way some people are, whatever the reason, and by taking pride in ourselves, we can take back the power that has been siphoned away from us, pick ourselves up, dust ourselves off, and move on. Let's get over it, already. The choice is ours.

As transgendered and transsexual people form their own decisions about who and what they are, as they deal with feelings of guilt or shame, as they struggle with the concept of pride in just being trans, they need to ask themselves three questions:

Did I choose to be transgendered?

If I could go back to my conception and change it, would I?

If I knew before my own child's birth that he or she would be transgendered and I could change it, would I?

My answers are no, no, and no.

Here's another question:

If I have made a gender transition, did I choose to do so?

My answer is yes.

All these questions reflect the concept of choice. As transpeople, we often relinquish our own ideas of choice and free will, allowing ourselves to become the victims of our birth. We like to say, "I didn't choose to be transgendered. I was born that way. It's not my fault. You should feel sorry for me, not hate me." Although it's true that none of us chooses to be trans, here are the unspoken messages we're sending when we say these things:

"I didn't choose to be transgendered *and if I had the choice, I would choose not to be. I was born that horrible way. It's not my fault that I'm a freak. You should feel sorry for me, not hate me, because I'm a poor, pathetic victim.*"

How much better it would sound, how much stronger we would feel, how much prouder we would be, and how much more power we would have if we said instead:

"I didn't choose to be transgendered *but I would choose it if I could. I was born that wonderful, fascinating way. It's not my fault that I lead such an interesting, unusual life. You should not feel sorry for me, and not hate me, because I'm not a victim or a freak, and I have a lot to teach you.*"

I didn't choose to be transgendered, but I did choose what I was going to do about it. People don't like to hear that. Nontranspeople don't like to hear it. It makes them angry because, for some reason, they seem to think that they should have control over what I do with my own body. Transpeople don't like to hear it because they're afraid that, if any part of being trans looks like a choice, we won't be able to receive insurance coverage for medical and therapeutic assistance. News flash: we don't get it now. And regardless of what benefits *should* be allowed to me as a transperson, I refuse to let anyone take away from me the idea that I have personal power, personal freedom, control of my own body, and the right to choose who I am and what I do.

When we deny that anything we are or do is a choice, we're giving up a great deal of personal power. We create a victim mentality that turns us into children at the hands of the larger society and the medical and psychiatric establishments. I don't need other people to decide when and if I should transition. I don't need to live my life around other people's time frames, decisions, and the misguided theory that they know what's best for me. I'm not a victim of my transness any more than I'm a victim of my brown eyes or my small feet. I control my life, and I control what I do with it. As long as we refuse to acknowledge personal power in our decisions—i.e., choice—we give up huge parts of ourselves to the control of others.

By the same token, we must take personal responsibility for our decisions. Because I made my own decisions, my therapist, my doctor, and anyone else involved in my transition is not to blame if everything isn't perfect at every moment. I can bemoan the fact that a large part of society hates me or finds me disgusting, but I knew that before I transitioned and I made my choices possessing that information. I can bemoan the fact that it's difficult to find a partner, but I knew that as well. If I choose to come out in a culture that doesn't accept me, I make that decision knowing the rejection that might await me. My recourse—my responsibility—is to educate others in the hope that things will change for me and for the rest of the trans community in the future.

The most frightening thing about giving up our personal power and our concept of choice, about relegating ourselves to victimhood because we were "born this way," is that it invites the notion of and the necessity for a "cure" for our "condition." And what if a "cure" is found? What if scientists discover a "trans gene" or an "abnormal" brain region? If a cause for transgenderism is found, can a cure be far behind? We might eventually be able to determine, in the womb, whether or not a child is transgendered. What will this mean for us? It could mean that we will someday be able to "fix" a transgendered child even before he or she is born. Or if we can't, we can just get rid of that poor, pathetic freak before he or she has to suffer the consequences of a transgendered life. The ramifications of this are too terrifying to think about.

I don't want to be "cured." I'm glad I'm alive. I love who I am. It's not me who needs to change but society, our culture, our way of thinking about trans, gay, lesbian, and bisexual people. But as long as we allow ourselves to be victims, as long as we deny ourselves the power of our own choices, as long as we leave the unspoken words hanging in the air, we encourage our own infantilism by others and we encourage the cause-and-cure mentality that could do away with "our kind" forever. And that would set a very frightening precedent for dealing with diversity in the world.

The idea of having a choice is right up there with the uppity position of being proud of who we are—it makes people angry. But we all make choices every day. And choice equals personal power equals pride. As transpeople, we should never give up the power to make our own decisions to the extent that we can. Unfortunately, there is a world out there that would take that power away from us, sometimes in the guise of doing what's best for us, as if we aren't intelligent adults and can't possibly act in our own best interests. If we don't speak up, if we don't make ourselves visible and let our voices be heard, if we don't come out and let people know who we are, our lives, and our destinies, will continue to be decided for us. We'll continue to be discriminated against, receive substandard medical care, lose our jobs, our housing—even our lives. For transmen, who so easily assimilate into the mainstream male community due to the strength of testosterone, the temptation to disappear can be overwhelming. To be "out" is to risk everything. But that will never change if we make ourselves scarce.

As female-to-males, we can do even more for ourselves and for our community by coming out. The majority of nontranspeople still don't know what a female-to-male transsexual is. Many assume that transsexuality is a phenomenon found in the male-born population only. Although some of us might find that a relief, because people don't look too closely at us that way, in fact it can serve to keep us down. If we are few and far between, why bother providing services for us? Why bother publishing our books, presenting our opinions, showing us representations of ourselves in the media? Why train medical students about us, why prepare those going into the gynecological field? We often do ourselves more damage by remaining in the closet.

And by coming out, we can also help our trans sisters. When society sees that this is not some deficiency affixed to the Y chromosome, but something that is shared throughout the population —every population in the world—we might all be able to achieve greater acceptance and inclusion.

When I first began my transition, I fancied myself a man and saw my future as one of adaptation to and assimilation into traditional male roles and identity. However, my resolve to quietly enter manhood and remain there lasted about as long as my first dose of testosterone. I come from rather politically rebellious roots—my parents staged a sit-in long before there was a name for such a thing, in the early 1950s, in order to integrate a Nebraska hotel. They spoke their minds, championed the civil rights of all people, and let their liberal politics be known.

Although they are both long dead, I knew that they wouldn't sit back and let the civil liberties of any group be trampled on without speaking out and attempting to educate others. I knew that, no matter how comfortable it might be in the closet, it would be a tight fit, and I tend to be claustrophobic. And I also knew that transsexual people would never be recognized, would never be given the basic human rights that others take for granted, and would never be understood unless some of us were willing to speak out, to be heard, and to teach others about us.

I accepted the challenge and now write and speak about trans-sexual issues in a variety of venues—and that's where the pride comes in. It's difficult to get up in front of a group of people and talk about anything, especially yourself, without a measure of pride in who you are and what you stand for. I found this pride early on in my transition and it has never left me.

The lure of assimilation can be difficult to resist. For most transpeople, being a "normal," everyday man or woman has been a lifelong dream. The assumption carried around by so many non-transpeople—that transpeople are a little edgy, a little funky, a little eccentric, and even a little bizarre—doesn't hold up when applied to the majority of trans lives. Most nontranspeople would be surprised to learn how many of their suburban neighbors, their PTA committee members, and their church bake sale organizers are, in fact, transsexuals who have assimilated into mainstream het-erosexual society.

And because transsexuals can be denied so many basic human rights just because of who we are, and because we risk verbal and physical attack on a daily basis, who can blame those who just want to "blend in" and get on with their lives? The only problem with assimilation is that it doesn't change things. Transsexuals who as-similate often continue to live in fear, a fear greater than those who are out, active, and vocal about their transsexuality and their struggle for dignity and civil rights. It's not that assimilated trans-sexuals are living a lie—they are living their lives as the people they were meant to be and have become. But the fear of discovery, the fear of being accused of betrayal, the fear of losing everything that they have established for themselves, can engulf them in a cloud of shame and terror. Having to watch every movement, to burn every old photograph, to censor themselves before they speak, to turn away from an old friend in a restaurant for fear of being outed—these are heavy burdens to carry around day to day. And it's society that hangs these burdens like yokes around the necks of transpeople who only want to live like everyone else.

I stumbled upon my first gay pride parade quite by accident. I was still female and still in denial of my own transgenderism and any sexual orientation issues that status might bring up. My only purpose for going to the park was to get a tan, but as I spread my towel on the grass, it was hard not to notice that people were gathering in a large and festive group, and they certainly weren't there to look at my pasty white legs. I asked a woman what was happening. "It's gay pride day," she announced, with a look that said, "What cave have you been living in?" Up until that time, I was unaware that a "gay pride day" even existed, but I love a parade, so I stayed and watched, just for the fun of it. And it was fun.

I had never seen so many happy—no, downright joyous—people in my life. I had never seen so many colorful costumes, so many decorative floats, and so much diversity, from leather and motorcycles to ball gowns and high heels. I was hooked. I went home two hours later, humming "If My Friends Could See Me Now" and wondering a little at my overblown fascination with it all. It would be seven years and seven pride parades later that I would finally come to terms with my own gender and sexuality issues. Once I did, I came out with a vengeance. But, hey, I had good role models —entire parades of them, people so proud of who they were and the larger picture they stood for that they were marching down the streets of Denver announcing themselves to anyone who cared to look.

For transpeople, pride is just as important, although sometimes more elusive. Our numbers are smaller, our position in society more precarious, as even laws passed to include gay men and lesbians don't include us. We are hated sometimes, we are feared sometimes, and we are made fun of. But we exist, and we still have that right. We have a history and a community, one that has persevered against all odds and will continue to do so. And that's something that we can make the choice to be proud of.

CHanGInG THe PaTTerns

As soon as I began my transition, I started marching in the pride parade myself, waving one of the three homemade signs that I had concocted—"Support Your Local Transman," "Testosterone: Breakfast of Champions," and "Transmen Tie One On." For a period of time, I had great fun just being a transsexual. The transition was exciting, I was going through a male puberty in middle age, and I no longer had to restrict myself to socially sanctioned gender roles and expectations.

Many transmen, regardless of age, go through a period of adolescent thought and behavior brought on by body changes and the unfamiliar and overpowering sensations of testosterone. It levels out eventually, and the frightening thrill of change, the rabid sexual desires, and the adolescent silliness dissolve into real life. You still have to make a living and pay bills. You still have to interact with people in the world. You still have responsibilities, the expectations of others, and the day-to-day requirements of whatever life you have established for yourself. Regardless of how you feel inside or what you know to be true, the world sees you and responds to you as a man, and you have to figure out how to do "male" correctly, or at least acceptably, if you want to remain safe and maintain some semblance of the life you've already built.

But the remarkable thing about a gender transition is that you can add on to the foundation of your previous life or you can tear down the whole thing and start over from scratch. You can keep as much of yourself as you want and fling the rest of it into the wind. You can be—or you can become.

My dad had a saying for every event. None of them was original. He picked them up along the path of his life and pocketed them like a stealthy shoplifter, then brought them out at opportune times as if they were his own. I remember all of them and each one has some meaning for me, but one of my favorites was "Do what you've always done and you'll get what you've always gotten." The reverse, of course, is "If you want something different, do something different."

Transpeople, more than any other life-form, are allowed the opportunity to be reborn. We can literally start new lives at twenty, thirty, forty, or seventy. We get a second chance to live as we've always wanted to live and to be the person we've always dreamed of being.

Most people wallow through their lives relying on past experiences—some good, some bad—to shape their current reality. They want to change, but they can't. They're locked into the definition of self that they have created. They say, "I can't do that (stop overeating, play basketball, learn to fly an airplane) because it's just not like me." Or they say, "I've always been that way. I can't change now. I'm too old. It's too late." And they keep repeating the same damaging patterns or refuse to try something new because they're clinging to an image of who and what they are that doesn't include change.

Transpeople are change personified. We can, and do, reinvent ourselves, physically and otherwise. And the best thing about reinvention is that we don't have to be stuck where we were before. We can create entirely new beings out of the ashes of our former selves. Just because Terrence did things one way, there's no reason that Teresa has to. Paula might have felt one way about something

and Paul might feel entirely differently. We have the power to create from scratch the person we most want to be.

We have the power to change not only ourselves but others
as well. Whether it's through political action, marching in the
streets, voting, or just talking to someone one-on-one, we can
change minds. We can make things better for ourselves and for our
community. And we can become better people as a result.

So as we go about our metamorphosis, weeding through our
lives to discard what no longer has meaning and adding what's
most important, it's imperative that we remember how we came to
this place and to take some measure of pride in what we've accomplished for ourselves. To paraphrase my former therapist: "Our
surgical scars are the visible reminders of our battles as transpeople." Wear them well.

But with pride in ourselves and the optimistic view that we can,
eventually, change the climate of our culture comes responsibility
for others. We can't expect nonprejudicial treatment if we aren't
willing to give it ourselves. It starts within our own community. We
must reach out to transpeople who, for whatever reason, might not
have access to the information and services available—those on
fixed incomes, seniors, the differently abled, and those in rural
communities. We must be inclusive of minorities and attempt to
overcome language and cultural barriers in our outreach. We must
tear down some of the hierarchical structures that we've erected in
our community that say that those who are "fully transitioned" are
somehow better than those who have decided against surgical intervention, or that those on hormones are somehow more "legitimate" than those who aren't.

Then we need to go outside of our own community to join with
and support our allies and to fight discrimination wherever we
find it. There's no room for homophobia, racism, ageism, class-
ism, or any other kind of prejudice in our own movement or out-

side of it. We need to be visible in our support of civil rights for everyone, trans and nontrans alike, and become allies of other groups and movements. Hatred destroys. As we request that others keep an open mind about who we are, we must open our own minds and resist the urge to keep such a tight focus on our own issues that we fail to see what's going on around us.

About ten days after the World Trade Center attacks, I received an e-mail from a Middle Eastern country. No, surprisingly, it wasn't from their top-level government officials asking for my advice on how to proceed. It was, in fact, from a transgendered female asking for advice on how to get help with a gender transition. In his/her country, such things are nearly impossible. Unfortunately, in my country, such things are nearly impossible as well, and I could be of little help to this person, other than to refer him/her to a resource in the Middle East.

But the exchange was interesting because, amid everything that was happening in my country and in his/her own, the daily rigors of individual life, including dealing with gender issues, continued. The need for mind/body gender congruity is so strong that it outweighs other concerns, like personal safety, and other questions, like "Am I going to be alive tomorrow?"

This letter proved that, regardless of race, ethnicity, religion, nationality, or any of the dozen other markers that we use to divide us, we have similar issues, wants, desires, and dreams. And if we're not so different from people halfway across the globe, maybe we're not so different from our friends, neighbors, and community—both trans and nontrans—here at home.

PART SIX

POST Trans

A MAN IN THIS WORLD

For some transsexual people, there truly is a post trans—a period that begins when they believe they are integrated enough into their new gender to be a complete "man" or "woman" and ends when they die. They assimilate into their new gender, possibly marry and adopt children, and leave any trappings of their trans past behind. For me, there is no post trans. I will always be a transsexual. But there is definitely a post transition, and it's the space in which I now live, where I'm satisfied with the hormonal and surgical changes that have occurred, where I don't have to introduce myself as a transsexual to everyone I meet, and where I don't have to pretend that I'm not one, either.

I've struggled through the initial stages of transition. I've managed to moderate the overwhelming sex drive that began with my first testosterone shot, cultivate enough facial hair to please me, and come to accept that my basically hairless body is the genetic legacy left to me by my male forebears. Shaving's a hassle now, rather than something I look forward to. I've finally figured out an acceptable male wardrobe after much trial and error and a lot of expense for clothes I didn't like but thought that I should have as a man. Although some of my friends love to don a suit and tie as a visible presentation of their maleness, I can't tolerate the constriction and use my transness to justify wearing a T-shirt or an open collar underneath a blazer for dressy occasions. If I'm going to be a nonconformist, why not go all the way?

Although my chest will always be scarred, I've come to accept it as a part of me. My pants stuffer is most often found in my drawer instead of my drawers. I no longer turn, or even feel the urge to, when people say, "Ma'am. Oh, ma'am." I know they aren't talking to me. I've become invisible, just another guy on the street. I'm just living my life in the best way that I know how and trying to educate and entertain some people along the way. If I've done that, then it's been worth it.

Reviewing the pieces of my life since transition is a bit like looking at my naked baby pictures—some are really cute and some make me cringe. But what I notice most are the inconsistencies in my thought processes and opinions—unlike my baby pictures, where the only inconsistency seems to be that they are photographs of a baby girl. I struggled to fit in, then I struggled to come out. I wavered back and forth about my identity—not just what I was, but who I was. I changed my mind a lot, and I changed myself a lot. Since I consider myself fairly well adjusted, I can only draw the conclusion that this gender thing is a lot more confusing than I would like to believe and a lot more unusual than I generally think it is.

Someone recently asked me, "How do you see yourself as a man in this world?" Even after all the soul searching I've been through in the last few years—more than some people do in a lifetime—I still don't have a good answer for that. The answer I came up with, just to have a response, is that I don't see myself as a man in this world. I have no realistic idea of what it's like to be a man in this world. I also have no realistic idea of what it's like to be a woman, but I have a much better notion, having lived in that guise for so many years. I think that, as transsexuals, we have misplaced so many large chunks of ourselves, or they have been misplaced for us, that it's difficult to answer certain questions. We've been "cheated," in a way, in the socialization that we didn't get, in the peer group encounters that didn't happen for us, and in the life experience that grants other people membership in the "man" and "woman" clubs and sometimes leaves us on the outside with our noses pressed to the window.

I don't know the secret password to get in. I haven't decided yet if I even care. But I do know that, so far, I'm unable to come up with any good answers to a lot of the questions that I am asked, such as:

What made you feel like you should be a man? *I don't know.*

How do you feel different now? *I don't know.*

Do you feel like a man now? *I don't know.*

Are you happier now? *I don't know.*

How can you justify changing your gender just because you didn't feel right? *I don't have to justify it.*

Do you think you're better off now? *I don't know.*

Lame, elusive responses to legitimate questions from people really seeking to understand what they perceive as an alternate universe, and what I usually perceive as a normal state of existence. After more than a half decade of writing about this and thinking about this and living this, I still can't come up with any good, satisfying responses. But at least they're consistent.

When the band stops playing and the lights come up, you still have to go home with yourself. And since you and yourself are keeping steady company, you damn well better like who you're spending all your time with. If you can't accept the part of you (or the whole of you) that's trans, you'll pass a lot of time being miserable. Having to constantly cover up what you say or do out of fear of discovery can be a long and tiring endeavor.

But being a "professional transsexual" can be exhausting as well. There are times when I just want to walk away at the end of the day and hang up my transness like a McDonald's employee hangs up his or her uniform. Even a conversation about the weather would be a welcome relief. If I don't come out to someone right away, or ever, it's not because I'm ashamed of myself or who I am. It's not because I want to trick people, betray them, or keep a secret from them. It's because I want to talk to them about literature or art or music or politics or movies or even what they want for dinner. I want to hear about who they are and I want them to see who I am, underneath the trans body and all that goes with it. With that in mind, when I do come out to someone, I want him or her to feel free to ask away—and then I want to talk about the weather.

Even though I have, so far, decided not to adopt a post-trans identity that includes ceasing to identify as a transsexual and slipping quietly into the mainstream of society, there are still many adjustments I've had to make because of my appearance. Society expects different things from its males than it does from its females, and getting used to that has probably been the most difficult part of the whole journey.

In the beginning, I trained myself to do things that were foreign to me, such as opening doors for women and standing when I'm introduced to someone. I learned how to give a firm handshake while making eye contact and to get drinks for female companions at parties. I learned how to stand with my legs apart, my body centered, my weight evenly distributed, as if I'm standing at a urinal at all times.

These things come naturally to me now, but there was a clumsy education process that most guys go through at puberty or before, with at least one male role model to help. Some nontranspeople are surprised that these things don't come naturally to transsexual people, but socialization is a powerful persuader, and I was definitely socialized as a female. Becoming a self-taught male in middle age has been an interesting, and enlightening, experience.

One of the most curious, and disturbing, developments of being male in the world has been the almost palpable fear of some women who encounter a man on the street, especially after dark. There are women who clutch their purses tightly when they pass me, as if I'm going to snatch them. Some women, at night, will cross the street when they see me coming, as if I'm going to snatch *them*. This might be flattering, knowing that I'm so fully perceived as male, if it weren't so confusing, offensive, and, well, sad. Reflected in the fear and uncertainty of these behaviors is a part of manhood that I want no part of. I hate that women don't feel safe to walk on the street, and I hate that *any* woman doesn't feel safe around me. Having been where they are, I understand the apprehension. And being where I am now, I understand that it needs to be stopped, and that men have the power to stop it—in many ways.

Shortly after the terrorist attacks in the United States, there was a major brouhaha in Boulder, Colorado, involving the Boulder Public Library and the American flag. It seemed that the library sponsored an art exhibit by Boulder Safehouse, a battered women's shelter, entitled "Art Triumphs over Domestic Violence." Included in the exhibit was a piece that featured ceramic penises of various colors strung up on a clothesline. The piece was called "Hanging 'Em Out to Dry."

These colorful penises apparently hung without comment in the library for several weeks, but a problem arose when an employee asked about hanging a giant American flag over the library's outer door. When the head librarian refused, saying that it might alienate some people given the current political climate, and pointing out that American flags were displayed elsewhere in the building, a controversy ensued. That controversy came to a head when a "thief" somehow removed the penises in protest. The dangling organs were later recovered unharmed, and the self-proclaimed "dildo bandit" turned himself in. He said that he was only trying to make a statement about the importance of hanging the flag as opposed to stringing up a bunch of phalluses in a place that is often frequented by children.

Much fuss was made of the unpatriotic head librarian, the suddenly obscene artwork, and the innocent little minds that could forever be traumatized by such a blatant display of disembodied male organs. Editorials were written and radio talk show hosts had a field day. Two camps were formed—those who were shocked that a dick display that had gone unnoticed for weeks was allowed to hang in the library when the flag was not, and those who believed that the rod wrangler was violating Safehouse's freedom of speech by removing the dismembered members.

Unfortunately, no one seemed to address the real problem, which, in my opinion, had nothing to do with the American flag and everything to do with why penises, and by association, their owners, are seen as symbols of violence that need to be "hung out to dry." I'm not saying that the artwork was wrong. What I *am* saying is that we need some dialogue here—men and women talking about why the artist and other women who supported the artwork feel that men need to be strung up.

Believe me, I'm well aware of the pain, fear, physical injury, and even loss of life that occur in a battering situation. What concerns me is that art is symbolic, and the ceramic penises are obviously a symbol for men in general. Some of the men I heard discussing this issue were outraged that the library rejected the American flag but hung the penises.

And they should be outraged, but not for that reason. Their outrage should come from the fact that some of their brothers have caused some women such misery that those women felt it necessary to symbolically dismember men. They should be outraged that someone has hurt these women so much that they express themselves with art that is undeniably anti-male. They should be outraged enough to open up a dialogue with women, to show women that men can be trusted, that they aren't cruel and vicious and hurtful, and that penises aren't the problem. And they should be outraged enough to tell their battering brothers that enough is enough and then do something about it.

At the time this whole controversy was occurring, we in the United States were expressing our outrage at how members of the Taliban were treating the women of Afghanistan. Our politicians were self-righteously spouting about the abuses that the Afghan women had suffered, and how we wanted to change it, to give these women back their rights and their dignity. We should have been, and still should be, equally appalled that the women of our own country feel the need to display hanging phalluses as a symbol of their anger and fear. Patriotism wasn't at issue here. The hate, hurt, anger, and disenfranchisement of battered women are the issues, then and now. Wake up, men of America—oh, and check your underwear.

There are a lot of excuses that violent men can give for their behavior toward women—the aggressive nature of testosterone (sorry, guys, I'm on it, too—that one doesn't fly), their socialization, the (almost) unlimited power that men are given in our culture, and the fear and anger that arise whenever that power is threatened—but none of these are valid. We aren't "opposite" genders. I know that now, having lived as both female and male and having interacted with the world in both genders. We are more alike than different, and we need to stop living on different planets and start living on earth, together. It's not difficult. Look for the gender-diverse people of this world—we'll show you the way.

I DO. can you?

Most people who have chosen a post-trans identity and assimilated into mainstream culture want all the trappings of that culture—including marriage. Yes, transpeople do fall in love, and
many want to express their commitment to their partner in the
most socially revered and acceptable way, and most have been able
to do so. But there are some who have not, and there are others
who have had wills, insurance policies, and other legal documents
involving spouses challenged and invalidated, leaving either the
transperson or his or her spouse without recourse. In the ongoing
controversy about "same-sex marriage," transpeople have pretty
much been ignored, but we need to take up the battle cry and join
with gay men and lesbians—not only for our own benefit, but for
the benefit of all human beings who are treated as second-class
citizens under the law.

Our government is known for spending a lot of time on the
really important things, like prohibiting same-sex marriage, while
ignoring the minor dramas of children without health care, adults
without jobs, and families without homes. It seems to me that if
the right wing really wants to torment gay men and lesbians, they
should let them get married. Then they can be as miserable as
everyone else. Anyone who actually *wants* to participate in an institution that fails at least 50 percent of the time should at least
have a go at trying to make it better. But the truth is that marriage

not only encompasses a visible, socially sanctioned way of expressing love and commitment, it also entails hundreds of benefits that protect spouses and children—benefits that gay and lesbian couples are not entitled to, even under domestic partnership regulations.

The trans community actually holds some pretty interesting pieces to the puzzle in this continuing battle about who should have basic human rights and who should not. We can make a mockery of any "Defense of Marriage" act or any state or federal constitutional amendments that are floating around attempting to deny honest, taxpaying citizens a piece of their humanity. However, no one has asked us. No one has included us. As of this writing, none of the major GLBT political organizations, most of which are quite T inclusive in other areas, has even mentioned us in this context. Intersexed people could be pretty formidable allies in this issue as well, but I haven't seen them mentioned either.

The reality is that no matter what laws are put into place to prevent gay men and lesbians from expressing what our society considers to be the highest form of love and commitment, transpeople, whether assimilated or not, will make sure that there are "gay marriages." No matter how those who support marriage as "a union between a man and a woman" decide to define those terms—*man* and *woman*—the "gay marriages" they want to prevent will take place. It simply depends on how *man* and *woman* are defined.

If the terms are defined by chromosomes, then almost every transman in existence can marry a man. We all have an XX chromosome. In most cases, under this definition, two hairy-faced men with "M" on their driver's licenses would be able to legally marry. Sounds like a "gay marriage" to me. And the same would hold true for transwomen. They would be free to marry women, based on their chromosomes. Two bridal gowns coming down the aisle—what a beautiful sight, and all perfectly legal.

If the terms are defined by genitalia, it would still leave a lot of room for two tuxes or two gowns. Because many transpeople, both male and female, don't have genital surgery, no matter how masculine a transman might appear, he could still marry a man, and the most feminine of transwomen could marry a woman, provided they still have their original genitalia. The same is true if the terms are defined by sex at birth.

And if *man* and *woman* are defined by current papers, or by how a person presents him- or herself in the world, there will still be plenty of "same-sex" marriages. Even if a transman has had genital surgery, he still has an XX chromosome, which our culture uses as the ultimate determination of male and female. If he marries a woman, which he is likely to do, since many more transmen identify as heterosexual than homosexual, we still have a marriage of two people with XX chromosomes—a same-sex marriage. The same is true of transwomen. If a transwoman marries a man, it will be a marriage of two people with XY chromosomes.

And none of this even touches on intersexed people, who have various physical makeups, chromosomal structures, and genitalia. Are they not to marry at all?

In this diverse world, no matter how much some people want to make things black and white, left and right, male and female, there are forces to be reckoned with that refuse to play by these rules. People in love can be forbidden to marry, but that won't stop them from being in love. Transpeople can assimilate into mainstream society, but that won't stop some of us from transgressing the boundaries our society sets up. We will get married, and we will raise families, and we will live our lives the way *we* decide to.

Thousands of transpeople were married at the time of transition. In many cases, these marriages were legally and unintentionally transformed into same-sex marriages. Yet they continue to thrive. And they haven't had any effect on mainstream heterosexual marriage at all. Thousands more have married after transition. Depending on state laws, many of these marriages could be legally considered same-sex marriages. Last time I looked, heterosexual marriages were still going strong—at least 50 percent of the time. None of these transsexual marriages, even those that could actually be considered same-sex marriages, has destroyed the institution of marriage in any way.

Those who fear that same-sex marriage will somehow have a negative effect on their own marriage must have a pretty shaky commitment. It seems to me that a strong, healthy marriage would survive regardless of the genders of the couple next door. But those who are worried about it can take a look at all the successful trans marriages out there—marriages that existed long before the current uproar—to see that a union between any two people in love will only make the institution stronger and more viable.

Because transpeople can lay waste to just about any marriage rule or regulation that's written into law, we are essential voices in the same-sex marriage debate. There is no way that any definition of marriage, or of man and woman, will keep same-sex marriages from happening—transpeople, by their very nature, will see to that. So the point is moot, and the best course of action for those who are worried that same-sex marriage will somehow damage their own is to quit spending their time introducing legislation and spend some time instead with their spouse and children. A simple act like that is what will maintain the sanctity of marriage—that, and allowing others who want to make the same commitment to do so.

The commitment to marriage is what will keep the institution strong. And transpeople will continue to make that commitment, if the stack of wedding invitations I receive from my friends every year is any indication. The one thing that society shouldn't be trying to prevent at this time in history is love.

WHaT NOW?

It was several years after my transition that I decided to change my birth certificate. I resisted as long as possible, but then a friend and I decided to go to Europe, and I had no choice. I needed to get a passport, and it would have been impossible to travel looking the way I do with a passport that said "Female." Even now, I go through bouts of regret about having changed the record of my birth. It's almost like denying that I was ever born at all.

For me, the person who exists now is not the person who was born in a small Midwestern city so long ago. That person was a female with a different name. And that person was reflected on that birth certificate. So when I changed it, it was almost like wiping her off the face of the earth. I don't want to do that, because that person isn't dead. That person is in me. That person is a part of me. And although that person isn't exactly me, I'm quite fond of her. For that reason, I haven't destroyed pictures of her or mementos that prove that she lived—that I lived, in another time, place, and form. I have good memories of the first part of my life, even though it sometimes seems as if someone else lived it, and I don't want to throw that away. I was born a female and denying it doesn't change that. Seeing my new male birth certificate was a very moving and bittersweet experience. Had I been given any other choice, had I even been allowed to choose a neutral gender or put "transsexual" on the certificate, I might have taken this option. But there are no such options in this world. I am either/or.

There are many transsexual people who eliminate their pasts. This is, in my opinion, an outdated recommendation that some very traditional therapists and support organizations still champion. These people are told to get rid of all photographs, change all documents, and destroy any and all evidence indicating that, before transition, they existed at all. They are even told to make up a past life to go with their new identity. I take issue with advising any person, but especially someone middle-aged or older, to deny over half a life. Regardless of the quality of that life, it had an effect on the person who lived it. It molded and shaped that person in many ways. Ridding oneself of one's past might allow a person to move into the post-trans, assimilated identity to which so many aspire, but to deny a former existence is to deny a large part of oneself. It might work for some, but it would never work for me.

The most beautiful thing about being a transsexual person is being able to experience the world in two genders. This is true for all of us, regardless of how we perceive ourselves and our gender identification. We have all faced the world in two genders, and we have the gift of being able to share our experiences and the insight that we've gained simply from living our lives. Those of us who embody both genders, who have taken the masculine and feminine parts of ourselves and put them together, can be especially helpful in teaching others, both trans and nontrans, to accept, integrate, and cherish both the masculine and the feminine in people and in the universe.

There's something about the blending of the two genders that takes on an almost spiritual quality, and that certainly causes appreciation of the world from two different points of view. With this knowledge and this experience, we can work toward healing divisions between men and women—divisions that have no purpose and no need to exist—and end the curse that has been inflicted on our world by the establishment of "opposite" genders. But we can do this only if we first acknowledge who we are.

Instead of reeling from our pasts, instead of cursing our fate and our misfortune, we can embrace the gift that we were given and use it to our advantage. There's a world out there that could mightily benefit from what we have to offer, and that in and of itself might be the reason that we exist. Forget causes. Forget cures. It might all be in some larger plan, and who are we, and who is anyone else, to say differently?

No matter what my birth certificate says, a female baby was born to my parents, and that life didn't disappear the day I decided to transition. And I believe that when I die, my death certificate will probably say "Female." Most coroners, it seems, are not too hip when it comes to the whole transsexual thing. The only record of my life on earth as a transsexual man will be in what I leave behind. But I don't remember being born and I'm not going to remember dying, so the thing that really matters is what I did with the life I was given in between those two events. I'm still working on it.

A Trans-Friendly World

To transpeople, the world can sometimes seem uninviting, hostile—even terrifying. But that hasn't stopped us, and it won't. Most transpeople are very determined to be the people they were meant to be, just as anyone else is. The tacky tabloids and the Hollywood scriptwriters often like to portray us as sex offenders or murderers—or at the very least, oddly unstable. But this is not reality.

Most transpeople who make the decision to transition just want to get through it and get on with their lives, whether they assimilate into the mainstream community or become activists for the civil rights to which we, like all people, are entitled. But no matter how we choose to live out our lives after transition, there are things that can be done, both by individuals and by society as a whole, that can make the world a more open and friendly place for transgendered and transsexual people. Will they be done? Maybe not in my lifetime. But with education and understanding comes change, and the best I can do is make some suggestions and hope that someday everybody catches on.

The Bathroom Blues

For a newly transitioning transsexual, the public restroom is the closest thing to hell. I started sweating more when I started using testosterone, but I never sweat so much as I did when I had to use the restroom at a mall or restaurant at the beginning of my transition. Restroom use is probably the biggest single issue for a person transitioning on the job, and it's a major discussion point in any trans support group.

There are actually those who believe that transpeople use the restroom in order to spy on others or to get some kind of sexual thrill. What most nontranspeople don't realize is that the bathroom can be a terribly frightening place for transpeople and we usually want to get in, take care of business, and get out as quickly as possible. We have no interest in seeing or hearing what others are doing and we would rather not have anyone else see or hear what we're doing. Most transpeople, especially those who are new to transition, would prefer not to use public restrooms at all. I've known transpeople who have refused liquid all day in order to avoid the restroom. Trust me when I say that we are there for one purpose only, just like everyone else is, and that we have no ulterior motives.

This particular aspect of transition seems to be much harder on male-to-females. Transmen, once we get over our initial concerns about using a stall instead of the urinal, about which way our feet are pointing, and about what our urine sounds like when hitting the bowl, generally fare pretty well. I used to float toilet paper in the bowl to muffle the sound of liquid smacking into liquid, but I soon learned that everybody sounds about the same when they pee, that many men prefer to sit on the toilet even when they don't have to, and that men in general try to pay as little attention as possible to other men in the restroom.

Smiling at the person standing next to you at the sink, so common among women when they are brought together by fate and a mutual biological need, can wreak havoc in the men's room. It apparently signals only one thing, with two very different outcomes —an immediate date in an adjoining stall or a black eye, the latter being much more likely. Since I was neither a lover nor a fighter at the beginning of my transition, I learned to lose the smile and stop acknowledging the other men at all. Men are goal oriented, and in most public restrooms, there is only one goal. So I taught myself to look straight ahead, take care of business, and get on with life, and I did just fine. Certainly there are major dangers for a transman if his gender status is discovered—assault or rape come to mind—but after a few months on testosterone, most transmen arouse little suspicion, especially if they simply act as if they belong there. We do belong there, after all.

Transwomen, on the other hand, can cause quite a calamity. A transwoman whose papers are not yet changed to reflect her new gender can risk arrest, and even those whose identification has been corrected can be subject to harassment and complaints from other female patrons. If a transwoman is especially tall or large, or in some other way stands out, she can quickly draw attention to herself. It's unfortunate that the general public is not yet educated enough in these issues to understand. A transwoman, regardless of her papers, can hardly use the men's room in a dress and high heels. And even coworkers seem to turn what could be uneventful elimination into a major workplace upheaval. The truth is that sex and gender really don't matter when fulfilling the basic urge to pee, and my advice to those who think we're in the restroom for any other reason is: don't flatter yourself.

A truly trans-friendly world would have unisex restrooms—not just here and there, but in every building that was required to have a restroom at all. There could still be men's and women's rooms for those stuffy people who define themselves by their genitalia, but a unisex restroom could solve a host of problems. The ones I have been in are usually just one room, with a sink, a toilet, and sometimes a urinal. And they're not just for transsexuals anymore—anyone who wants a modicum of privacy welcomes the single-occupant unisex bathroom, where the differently abled can find space and comfortable accommodations, where those who need to change clothes or colostomy bags can find refuge. Even those who are simply pee shy appreciate the solitude. This doesn't mean that all transsexuals will use the unisex restroom, even if it's offered. And they shouldn't have to. But it's a great place for those whose papers don't match their persona, or for those who just welcome a little extra privacy. And if nontranspeople are terrorized by transpeople in "their" bathroom, they could always use the unisex room as well.

THOSE PESKY Pronouns

I have, on occasion, been called "it." Not only is it not funny, it's a guarantee that the person who says it is not worthy of my time. Ignorance isn't something I generally bother with. But pronouns can be problematic, for both trans- and nontranspeople. There's nothing more annoying, and sometimes downright hurtful, to a transsexual person than the incorrect use of a name or pronoun. In the beginning of a transition, it's very difficult for others to make the switch and people sometimes slip up. But if they continue to use the pronoun "she" long after a transman has grown a full beard, or if they continue to refer to Nancy as Ned several years after she has transitioned, they're in danger of completely alienating that person (if they haven't done so already). The friendship or relationship is at stake, and only those interacting with the transperson can decide if they value it enough to make the necessary changes in their thought processes.

What I found in questioning my friends and coworkers who easily made the adjustment and those who did not (and are still having trouble) is that those who were able to make the switch with little problem had made the decision to see me as an entirely different person—a male. One coworker said that she pretended that I was my own brother, and she never made a mistake with my name or my pronoun. Those who constantly slip up, even after many years, are those who decided that I was still a female, but one that they would now have to refer to as "he" and "him." Even though I have a mustache and a goatee, no breasts, wear male clothing, and am referred to as "he" by everyone else in the world, these few people continue to use the female pronoun. They have not been able to make the switch. My only revenge is that they look like fools in public when they use "she" to refer to me and no one else knows who they're talking about. I can always roll my eyes, shake my head, and give the waiter or salesclerk a secret smile to let him or her know how sorry I feel for someone who can't tell a man from a woman.

In all seriousness, however, to be unable to make this change signifies a lack of respect for a trans friend or loved one. I forgive children and, usually, parents, for whom the transition might be so traumatic that it's impossible for them to fully adjust. I'm less patient with friends and coworkers. When I hear things such as, "Oh, I'll never get that pronoun right," what it says to me is that these people have no intention of trying, that they don't care enough for me to even make the effort. They've already given up. When I hear, "You'll always be female to me," what it says is that this person has no idea who I really am and couldn't care less. With the limited amount of time I have on earth, why would I choose to spend it with people who don't want to know or acknowledge who I am?

In all fairness, though, even transpeople mess up sometimes—although we'll never admit it. There have been a handful of times when I've stopped just short of referring to myself as "she" when I'm talking about myself in the third person. Once in a while, I'm still female in my dreams, which seemed to evolve just like my "passing" did—I was male 25 percent of the time in my dreams, then 50 percent, and so on. But it still hasn't reached all male, all the time—and maybe it never will. I generally keep that to myself, especially if I want to get annoyed with someone else who calls me "she." May the day never come when I expect the same of myself that I do of others.

But it's not just the one-on-one pronoun use that's problematic. No matter how we identify, every form we fill out forces us to choose. I much prefer a fill-in-the-blank form, where we can all decide our own gender. There's more of a choice now for ethnic background than ever before, but many people still have to check "other," and nobody likes to be an "other." A fill-in-the-blank form would remedy this insult as well. Once society stops putting people in little boxes for its own convenience, we'll all be able to recognize the true and beautiful diversity that's out there. And maybe we'll stop thinking about each other as "other" and realize that we're all human beings.

on-the-job jitters

The most trans-friendly thing that an employer can do for people who are transitioning on the job is to not fire them. Once that's decided, there are some things that can be done to make an on-the-job transition go smoothly.

It's important for a transperson to come up with a plan that he or she can present to an employer. That plan should include how and when coworkers and clients will be told, how any bathroom issues will be resolved, what time off will be needed and when, a time frame for name change, wardrobe change, and change of pronoun usage, and a time frame for visible physical changes, if they will affect the transperson's interaction with others (clients, for example). The plan should be flexible and should be reworked, if necessary, with the employer's input.

It might sound like an invasion of a transperson's privacy to be so detailed, but in most states, there are no protections at all for transpeople, and they can be easily fired with no recourse. Because of this, it's essential for the transperson to make this transition as easy as possible for the employer. With a plan already in place, the employer doesn't have to worry about details. The employer should be assured that business will continue as usual. The transperson should make every effort to cause as little disruption as possible to the work environment. This isn't a time to make demands. Jobs are hard to come by. So are good employees. If both sides can be flexible, an on-the-job transition will go smoothly and successfully.

Transpeople should be aware, however, that there are some states or cities (very few) in which they are protected. They should also be aware that certain questions or actions are illegal, no matter what. Transpeople are under no obligation to discuss their surgeries. Sick leave is sick leave, and if a note from a doctor is required, the doctor performing surgery can write a generic letter. No transperson should be questioned about his or her genitalia. The only concerns involved in a transition should be whether or not anything will affect the transperson's ability to do his or her job. Transpeople who feel that their employer has acted illegally should contact an attorney or a legal assistance program.

A well-informed employer and workforce can make for a comfortable transition. Some employers are so skittish that they simply don't want to deal with the situation. Maybe if they ignore it, it will go away. It won't. The transition will forge right ahead without them, and coworkers will be left to gossip and worry about what's happening, allowing for constant workplace disruption.

Some transpeople are skittish, too. I was guilty of waiting far too long to inform my staff and my coworkers, but it actually worked in my favor. When I cut off all my hair and quit wearing makeup, the rumor mill decided that I had either cancer or AIDS. By the time I finally did inform people, they were so relieved that I wasn't ill that they were ready to accept just about anything.

The best thing to do, if possible, is to call in a trainer or consultant who can educate the workforce on trans issues and prepare them for the changes they'll see in their coworker. Some trans-people are comfortable doing this themselves, but many are not, and some choose to take a few days off while the training is going on, then return with their new name, pronoun, and appearance. The staff usually takes its cues from management, and if management is clear at the training that it supports the transperson and that any harassment will be disciplined, almost everyone will eventually come to support the transition—and if they don't, they'll keep it to themselves.

trans etiquette

I'm not going to call myself Emily Post here. I don't look a thing like her. But a trans-friendly home, workplace, or society ob-serves several rules of etiquette that are designed to cause the least offense possible and to make everyone feel more comfortable.

The most polite and respectful thing to do when interacting with anyone, trans or not, is to find out who that person is and accept it. In the case of a transperson, acceptance means using the name the person has chosen, the correct pronoun ("he" for FtMs, "she" for MtFs), the correct references ("brother" for an FtM sib-ling, "son" for an FtM child), and respecting that person's wishes with regard to how, or if, he or she wants others to know about the transition.

Everyone slips up. Even transpeople sometimes slip up with each other. But those slipups can be handled gracefully with a lit-tle thought and care. If the wrong name or pronoun slips out when speaking one-on-one with a transperson, the best response is usually "Oh, I'm sorry. I meant 'he' " or "I meant 'Steve.' " Then move on. In the company of others, especially those who don't know that the person is trans, it's best to let the mistake go by en-tirely and use the correct name or pronoun the next time it comes up. Most people won't notice, especially if they've already formed their idea of the transperson's identity. Panicking or drawing attention to the mistake can actually make things worse. Ongoing apologies are uncomfortable to everyone around and make the transperson the center of attention, which some of us love, but which most of us would rather avoid.

When doing business or interacting with a stranger who appears to be trans, the most supportive thing to do is nothing at all. Winking, smiling, gushing with friendliness—all those things draw attention to the situation and are obvious to the transperson and everyone else around. If the person is obviously trans, he or she is usually aware that it's obvious and will appreciate the signs of respect and acceptance that go along with a normal, everyday interaction. He or she will be aware of the support and acceptance that's there by what is *not* said or done.

It's generally okay to ask a transperson—quietly and respectfully—what pronoun he or she uses if it's not obvious. Even I have done this before and I have yet to meet anyone who has been insulted. In fact, most people seem very appreciative of this little gesture, which says that I respect them and care about their feelings. But the standard rule is to use the pronoun of the gender the person is presenting. If someone who looks obviously male is in a dress, wig, and high heels, "she" is the appropriate pronoun every time. For a person born female, a masculine appearance and dress can sometimes go either way, but if the name is masculine, if there's any facial hair, or if there are any other clues to masculinity, "he" is the way to go. Sure, names like Pat, Kelly, Don, and Dawn can get us all messed up, but this is just the little bit of mystery that transpeople like adding to our lives.

There are two questions that are absolutely forbidden—"Have you had *the operation*?" and "Why did you do it?"

"Have you had *the operation*?" goes hand in hand with "Are you done?" Either assumes some kind of incompleteness, the possibility of a partial human being. There is no such thing as "the op-

eration." Transpeople go through many operations or no operations. There is no singular "the operation." We know what the
question means—"Did you have genital surgery?" But that's a
question that's necessary only in limited situations, and if that's
what a person wants to ask and thinks it's important to know, then
it needs to be asked straight out. No euphemisms. And the person
asking the question needs to consider whether he or she would
ask a nontransperson about genitalia in the same situation. When
someone asks me if I've had "the operation," I like to say, "Well, I
had my gall bladder out a few years ago." It usually puts an end
to most lines of questioning, unless the person is suffering from
gallstones him- or herself and now wants the full details to know
what to expect.

"Why did you do it?" is also inappropriate. It assumes that
there are a whole host of reasons that have nothing to do with gender incongruity, or that the transperson just woke up one morning and said, "Hmm, this might be fun." This is a question that's
best left for detectives when questioning a murderer. Transpeople
transition because they need to resolve gender issues that have no
other resolution. The majority "do it" because they will otherwise
die or live so miserable a life that it would be like death. Transpeople transition for the same reason that people with cancer get
chemotherapy—to live.

In an ideal world, there would be no need for trans etiquette—
simple etiquette, extended to all people, would do. But in an ideal
world, there would be no reason for this book. Transgendered and
transsexual people would be assumed to be just like everyone else,
and issues of gender diversity would be addressed along with other
diversity issues, like sexual orientation, race, ethnic heritage, and
physical abilities. Children would grow up understanding that
there are some people who just naturally don't fit into male and fe-

male molds, and people would be used to seeing a selection of genders or a fill-in-the-blank gender question on every form.

But that world has yet to come, and it will arrive only through the visibility of transpeople who are willing and able to show others our humanity. I've spoken to hundreds of college and university students and have heard pretty much the same thing with every class. Before they met me, they were afraid. Some of them hesitated to come to class on the day that I was presenting. They thought that I would be a freak or a monster. Instead, they were surprised and relieved to find out that I'm "normal." They left class with a great deal of information and, hopefully, a different attitude. And some of them will spread the word—this is how acceptance, and change, happens.

I understand why some transpeople can't be out. They're supporting families and can't risk the loss of a job. They live in a rural or conservative area where their safety or their life could be put in jeopardy. But those who can, should. And to put a new spin on an old cliché, those who can, teach. We need to be engaged in open, educational dialogue with others whenever possible. And then we need to take a break, put up our feet, and enjoy our lives—just like everyone else.

Afterword

It's Easter morning, a little over six years after I first started my
transition, and I'm meeting my sister, her husband, and my four-
year-old nephew for breakfast at a local café. We are not the kind
of family who puts on our Easter finery and goes out for brunch, so
I stumble out of bed, stick my head under the faucet to tame the
various cowlicks that cropped up during the night, pull on a sweat-
shirt and jeans, and head out, scruffy and unshaven.

The goal of the morning is for the Easter Bunny to arrive at my
nephew's house while we are all away having breakfast. In order for
this to happen, I have to finish eating before everyone else, excuse
myself to run an errand, and assure my nephew that I will meet up
with all of them later at their home. Then, while they finish their
meal, the scruffy and unshaven "Easter Bunny" will be hiding
the candy and toys for my nephew to find. But first we have to get
through breakfast.

My nephew has never known me as anyone but Uncle Matt.
Eventually he will come to realize that Uncle Matt doesn't appear
in any of his mother's childhood family photos. Instead, there will
be some strange, elusive aunt that he has never seen and that no
one talks about. This awareness will probably occur at about the
same time that he starts questioning the existence of a giant rab-
bit that actually comes to his house, breaks in without damaging
any doors or windows, and hides chocolate eggs and Hot Wheels

in his living room. I don't know what my sister will tell him—we've never discussed it. How she handles it will be completely up to her, since she never seems to take my advice on other important matters of child rearing. Even so, she's done a fantastic job with my nephew, and for now he seems satisfied with the reality of both Uncle Matt and the Easter Bunny.

My sister, on the other hand, has had her moments of doubt along the way. Losing her big sister was tough, especially after losing her parents in late adolescence and early adulthood, and we went along for a while with a minimum of contact. She refused to call me her brother when I still had boobs, which, in hindsight, makes quite a bit of sense. Even now, both of us seem a little uncomfortable with the term, although she tries to sputter it out when it's required. I will always be her big sister—now her really odd big sister—and to expect her to see me as a brother is probably asking the impossible. I certainly don't see her through the eyes of a big brother—far better that I am simply Uncle Matt to her son and that we don't push any other newly created familial titles.

But this morning, regardless of whatever else I am to her, I am the Easter Bunny, and that will serve to carry us through the meal. The problem is that she's just stumbled out of bed herself—she is pale faced, disheveled, and tired enough that crankiness is hovering over her like a small rain cloud waiting to burst.

And when her over-medium eggs arrive, they aren't right. They're too runny—as runny as mine, which are over-easy. So we signal Brianna, our server, who is possibly a college student at the nearby university and who, like the rest of us, appears to have struggled against the alarm clock. Her hair is tied back haphazardly, her face is freshly scrubbed and featureless, and her manner says that she would prefer to be anywhere but working the Easter morning shift at this restaurant. But she forces a smile and tries to find out the problem.

"My eggs are too runny," my sister points out. "I'd like to get some new ones."

Brianna checks her order pad, and we discover that the customer is not always right at her station. "But you ordered them over-medium," she says. "That's over-medium."

"No," my sister counters. "I've had them here before over-medium and they weren't this runny."

At this point, the wisest thing for Brianna to do is to take the eggs back and return with a more solid offering. But she's not to be bested this morning, especially by a woman who seems frustratingly unintimidated.

"That's over-medium," Brianna says, pointing her pencil toward my sister's plate. "That's the way we cook them."

But she underestimates my sister, who has raised a child from a crabby and sleepless infancy through an overly inquisitive and sleepless toddler stage to the energetic and willful specimen sitting next to her now. Arguments don't deter my sister—they only make her stronger.

"But these are like *hers*," my sister says, flailing her arm in the direction of the plate of eggs directly across from her—my plate. "*She* ordered over-easy, and my eggs are runny, like *hers*."

Brianna looks at my plate. Then she looks at me. Then she looks at my sister, and I can sense a slight unease moving across her face.

"Like *hers*," my sister persists, seemingly intent on making a point. "My eggs are too runny. They're like *hers*."

Brianna blinks. My sister is adamant and gives no signal that she knows what she has just said. My nephew, too young to understand the universal but unspoken agreement that we all have with regard to pronouns, chews happily on his sausage link. My brother-in-law, a man of few words unless he's disagreeing with me, maintains his silence. It's time for me to step in.

"She means like these," I say calmly, motioning to my plate.

There are no more arguments. Brianna has decided, I believe, that my sister is unstable—possibly even dangerous. And she understands that there is some complicity here—that I, whoever I am, obviously know this woman well and am aware of her derangement. It's almost as if I had winked. *This is how we handle her. Just remain calm and play along.*

Brianna nods, scoops up the plate, and heads for the kitchen, returning a few minutes later with a different and firmer pair of eggs. In the meantime, my sister has apologized to me and blamed Brianna for this little pronoun fiasco because she instigated the argument. I'm truly unconcerned, because I'm not the one the entire waitstaff is whispering about as they congregate by the coffee machine.

In fact, I don't even have to stay and watch their eyes dart over to the table, then away, then back again. I get to walk away and deny that there is any common bloodline whatsoever between myself and the crazy woman at Table 5.

My sister has the correct set of eggs. Brianna has a story to tell when her shift is done and she goes home. I come away from the whole scenario looking perfectly normal. All's right with the world. I say my good-byes and slip quietly out the door, leaving my sister and Brianna to muddle over the importance of pronouns and the mystery of identity in the confusing, nontrans world in which they live. I have far more important things to worry about and far more important responsibilities to carry out.

After all, I *am* the Easter Bunny.

ACKnOWLeDGments

My life wouldn't be the same, and this book would never exist, without the help and support of so many people along the way. I know I'll forget some, and I apologize in advance. Thanks to Sean Gardner, De Edwards, Karen Whitfield, Kelley W., Rachael St. Claire, Susan Conder, Robynne Pennington and Carolee Laughton, Jessie Shafer, Philip Cherner and family, Ian Philips, Nicole Pool, Kevin and Don, Keith Lucero, Peter Clarke, Chris Kenry, Lake Lopez, Jerry Wheeler, Drew Wilson, Sean Wolfe, Lee Patton, Cheryl Allen, Karen Bryant, Nicole Dyk, Barbara Edwards, Evelyn Egan, Tom Greer, Natalie Ortler, Dawn Shields, Susan Wright, Duke Warren, Frank Lyon, Vince and Ashi, Malcolm H., Malcolm W., Jay W., Justin, Bonnie Bjornstad, Tama Kieves, Brad Furst, Kristi Miller, Linda Metsger, Bonnie Marcus, Jane Wampler, Bonnie Zare, Evelyn Haskell, Sharon Benson, everyone at the Gender Identity Center of Colorado, *Out Front Colorado*, and the Denver Gay Men's Book Discussion Group.

I would also like to thank my filmmaker, D. Robin Hammer, and her partner, Patty, for being so generous to me, and my band, Go Figure, for putting up with me—Michelle Ponikiski, Robert Nelson, Datti Kapella, Jamie MacCrimmon, and Tony Hamilton.

To my literary agent, Alison J. Picard, to my editor, Brian Halley, and to the staff of Beacon Press—thank you for believing in and supporting my work.

Trans-Lations

The transgendered community has created a language of its own, since none was previously available to help us describe our experience. If you ask five transpeople the meaning of a specific term, you will often get five different answers. The following definitions are generally accepted in the transgendered community. However, some definitions vary among certain people or groups, and this listing is only a beginning. It is presented here to help the non-trans reader understand my language and some of the references in the book and to make the trans reader aware of the meanings that I ascribe to the terms.

binary gender system: The two-gendered (masculine and feminine) system that exists in most cultures and that is based largely on genitalia.

bio-male/bio-female: Terms used to describe men who were born men and women who were born women, as opposed to people who have transitioned into a male or female body and identification. Preferred terms among many transpeople are *nontransmale* or *nontransfemale*.

birth sex: *See* sex.

chest surgery: The surgical reconstruction of the chest for female-to-male transsexuals to create a male chest, which can involve liposuction or a mastectomy, with or without nipple reconstruction. It can also be used to refer to breast augmentation surgery (implants) for male-to-female transsexuals.

crossdresser: A person who dresses in clothing of the "opposite" sex, usually for the purposes of relieving gender discomfort. In the past, this term has been used synonymously with *transvestite*, which has taken on negative connotations and is not often used in the trans community. Crossdressers are not drag queens. Drag queens are men who dress as women for stage performances. Drag kings are the female counterparts of drag queens. Some people who choose to perform drag might be transgendered, but performing in drag does not mean a person is transgendered, although drag queens and kings are often listed as part of the transgender community.

female-to-male (FtM): An individual assigned female at birth who identifies as male, either full- or part-time, and often dresses as male and assumes a male role in society. More specifically, it refers to a natal female who undergoes gender reassignment to male. Many natal females who have undergone such reassignment prefer either the term *transman* or *man*.

gender: Often used synonymously with *sex*, but actually more of a social construct, whereas sex is physical and biological. Gender defines roles, appearance, behaviors, and identity apart from physical sex characteristics. There is arguably a biological component to gender.

gender community: The community consisting of transgendered and transsexual individuals, as well as those who don't identify as either but present their gender in ways that don't conform to society's expectations for people of that gender.

gender diverse: An adjective used to describe a person or a person's appearance, behavior, or both, not conforming to accepted societal norms regarding male and female appearance and/or behavior. Another term that is often used interchangeably is *gender variant*, although many in the gender community reject the term because "variant" can have a connotation of abnormality.

gender dysphoria: The feeling of being at odds with one's body, genitalia, birth sex, and/or society's expectations of the roles and behaviors that coincide with the birth label of male or female. Many feel that this term carries a negative connotation as it suggests a psychological, rather than a physiological, basis for transgenderism. Gender Identity Disorder, a psychological diagnosis that appears in the *DSM* (the *Diagnostic and Statistical Manual* used by therapists to diagnose certain mental illnesses), is also disputed by many who believe that transgenderism is a medical condition, or that it is not a "condition" at all, but simply a way of being.

gender expression: The externalization of gender identity—clothing, hairstyles, hobbies, interests, behaviors, mannerisms, and other visible expressions of one's gender. This is also called *gender presentation*.

gender identity: The internal feelings and identification that individuals have with regard to being male or female. Gender identity includes how individuals feel about their physical bodies and their societal roles, expectations, and behaviors. Most people feel comfortable with their birth sex and the gender identification and most of the societal roles that go with it. Some people have a gender identity at odds with their bodies and the roles and behaviors that are expected of them.

Gender Identity Disorder: *See* gender dysphoria.

gender presentation: *See* gender expression.

gender reassignment: Correction of the body, through hormones, surgery, or both, to adhere to an individual's gender identity. Individuals who undergo these procedures are often referred to as transsexuals, although some reject that label and feel that once the procedures are complete and all identification papers are changed, they are members of the sex into which they have transitioned. *Sex change* is considered a somewhat dated term in the trans community, and most transsexuals will use the terms *gender reassignment, sex reassignment,* or, less frequently, *gender* or *sex correction.* Some prefer the term *gender reassignment,* believing that their social gender has changed, while others prefer the term *sex reassignment,* believing that their gender has always been the same and that they have corrected the physical body to match that gender. Many use the terms interchangeably.

gender transition: The process of outwardly moving from one gender to another through the use of hormones, surgery, or both, which includes such things as legal name change, change in identification papers, and change in clothing, appearance, mannerisms, and other identifying gender markers.

gender variant: *See* gender diverse.

genetic male/genetic female: *See* bio-male/bio-female.

GLB: Initials used to refer to the gay, lesbian, and bisexual community.

GLBT: Initials used to refer to the gay, lesbian, bisexual, and transgender community. Often other initials are added on, such as Q for queer, Q for questioning, and I for intersex.

hir: A gender-neutral pronoun that is a combination of "his" and "her"—for example, "hir book." Many people who do not identify as either male or female prefer to use gender-neutral pronouns to refer to themselves. *See also* nu *and* ze.

intersexed: Those who, at birth, exhibit some physical characteristics of both sexes or have ambiguous genitalia or chromosomal structures that differ from the "standard" XX and XY. When the genitalia of a newborn does not conform to the "standard" male and female genitalia most often seen, doctors and/or parents often choose (sometimes incorrectly) the sex to assign, and surgical procedures are initiated to correct the "problem." A movement is currently under way by adults who were born intersexed to leave intersexed children as born and allow these individuals to choose gender assignment and surgical procedures, if desired, at a later stage in life. Although it is up to each intersexed person to decide whether he or she chooses to identify as transgendered, intersexed people are often listed as part of the transgender community.

male-to-female (MtF): An individual assigned male at birth who identifies as female, either full- or part-time, and often dresses as female and assumes a female role in society. More specifically, it refers to a natal male who undergoes gender reassignment to female. Many natal males who have undergone such reassignment prefer either the term *transwoman* or *woman*.

natal male/natal female: *See* bio-male/bio-female.

natal sex: *See* sex.

nontransmale /nontransfemale: *See* bio-male/bio-female.

nu: A gender-neutral pronoun that is used in place of "he" or "she" or "him" or "her" by some people who do not identify as either male or female—for example, "Nu is reading the book now. The book belongs to nu." *See also* hir *and* ze.

phalloplasty: The operation used to surgically construct a penis for transmen.

sex: A person's biological and/or anatomical makeup, which can include chromosomes, genitalia, and secondary sex characteristics. *Birth sex, sex assignment,* and *natal sex* refer to the label of male or female given at birth and based on genitalia. The labels of male and female throughout life are based on primary and secondary physical sex characteristics and carry wide-ranging implications for their owners.

sex assignment: *See* sex.

sex change: *See* gender reassignment.

sex reassignment: *See* gender reassignment.

sexual orientation: A term used to refer to the sex and gender to which an individual is physically and emotionally attracted. This is not the same thing as gender identity, which refers to the sex and gender that an individual feels he or she is inside.

T: Has two distinct meanings in the trans community. It is used to designate the trans community as a whole, as in GLBT, and it is also used among transmen when referring to testosterone.

top surgery: *See* chest surgery.

trans: Used as a shortened version of transgendered and/or transsexual, and is sometimes used to designate anyone whose gender presentation does not match society's expectations for a person of that sex or gender.

transgender(ed) (TG): Most generally used as an umbrella term that encompasses a range of people. In general usage, it can refer to anyone who transgresses gender norms. More specifically, it is used to refer to people who experience discomfort and/or unhappiness, either some or all of the time, with their birth sex, including their anatomy, appearance, and expected social roles. The discomfort can be expressed in activities such as adopting the behavior and dress of the "opposite" sex, either full- or part-time; living in the role of the "opposite" sex, either full- or part-time; or physically altering the body through hormones and/or surgery (*see* gender reassignment and transsexual). It can also refer to those who present as androgynous or do not define themselves by gender at all. In some cases, these people self-identify as *genderqueer, genderless,* or *neutrois.* There are many other names that people use to define themselves.

transman/transwoman: *See* female-to-male and male-to-female.

transsexual (TS): Most commonly used to refer to an individual who has undergone gender reassignment that includes surgery and/or hormones, name change, change of birth certificate, and change of identifying papers—such as Social Security cards, diplomas, transcripts, passports, and so on. Many of these individuals have experienced such discomfort with their birth sex that they believe this is a life-saving procedure. The term can also be used to refer to an individual who is living full-time as a member of the "opposite" sex but has had no surgical or hormonal intervention. *Transexual* is an alternate spelling that some prefer.

ze: A gender-neutral pronoun that is used in place of "he" or "she" by some people who do not identify as either male or female—for example, "Ze is reading the book now." An alternate spelling is *zie.* *See also* hir *and* nu.

resources

There are many organizations available to help transgendered, transsexual, and gender-diverse people as well as their partners, family, and friends. Below are some of the most prominent. Most of the Web sites listed have links to other sites and other groups and organizations that can be of help as well.

FENWAY COMMUNITY HEALTH:
a Boston-based organization that works primarily on health care issues for the local GLBT community, but also runs a national toll-free GLBT helpline as well as the Peer Listening Line. Address: 7 Haviland Street, Boston, MA 02115; GLBT helpline: 888-340-4528; Peer Listening Line: 800-399-PEER; Web site: www.fenwayhealth.org.

FTM INTERNATIONAL (FTMI):
a long-standing international organization for female-born, male-identified persons. Address: 160 14th St., San Francisco, CA 94103; voice mail: 415-553-5987; Web site: www.ftmi.org.

GENDER EDUCATION AND ADVOCACY (GEA):
a national organization specifically focusing on the needs and rights of gender-variant people. Web site: www.gender.org.

GENDER IDENTITY CENTER (GIC) OF COLORADO:
a support, information, and referral organization for transgendered and transsexual people. Address: 1401 Saulsbury St.
#G-9, Lakewood, CO 80214; phone: 303-202-6466; Web site:
www.gicofcolo.org.

GENDERPAC (GPAC):
a Washington, DC-based political organization focusing on gender rights in general, including the rights of the gender diverse.
GenderPac hosts an annual conference. Address: 1743 Connecti-
cut Ave. NW, Washington, DC 20009-1108; phone: 202-462-
6610; Web site: www.gpac.org.

INTERNATIONAL FOUNDATION
FOR GENDER EDUCATION (IFGE):
since 1987, a leader in information and referral services focusing
on gender and transgender issues. IFGE publishes *Transgender
Tapestry* magazine. Address: P.O. Box 540229, Waltham, MA
02454; phone: 781-899-2212; Web site: www.ifge.org.

NATIONAL TRANSGENDER
ADVOCACY COALITION (NTAC):
a national organization working toward social and legal reform to
secure equal rights for transgendered and other gender-diverse
individuals. Address: P.O. Box 76027, Washington, DC 20013;
Web site: www.ntac.org.

PARENTS, FAMILY AND FRIENDS
OF LESBIANS AND GAYS (PFLAG):
an information and support organization for the loved ones
of GLBT people, with chapters in all fifty states. Web site:
www.pflag.org.

Transgender Law and
Policy Institute (TLPI):
a national organization dedicated to engaging in effective advocacy for transgender people in society.
Web site: www.transgenderlaw.org.